ENGLISH
TOOL
BOX

Karen Dawn Ryder

Professor, English Education, Hongik University
University of Paris VIII, France - B.A. in Plastic Arts & Western Philosophy
ST Giles College, San Francisco, USA — TEFL(Teaching English as a Foreign Language) graduate
Author, *Solomon TOEFL Speaking/Listening/Writing/Vocabulary*
Author, *TSE: Intensive Preparation for the Test of Spoken English*

English Toolbox

First published in 2025
By ECK Books
27, Changjeon-ro 2-gil, Mapo-gu, Seoul, Korea

Copyright©2025 by ECK Education, Inc.

Publisher   Seungbin Lim
Author   Karen Dawn Ryder
Director   ECK Content Lab
Editor   Hyunjin An
Design   SINGTA Design
Printed in Korea

Price 25,000 won
ISBN 979-11-6877-344-8   13740

www.eckbooks.kr
www.eckedu.com
eck@eckedu.com

ENGLISH TOOL BOX

The Perfect Guide to
Real-Life English Conversation

Karen Dawn Ryder

ECK Books

Preface

It is with great pleasure that ECK welcomes you to this intermediate course of English entitled, 'English Toolbox'. We warmly greet you all. This textbook has been specifically designed to train you in the necessary skills to consolidate, as well as expand, your knowledge of English. It will provide you with ample opportunities to put this knowledge to very practical use through multiple and diverse speaking activities.

Here at ECK, we know very well that learning a new language is not always an easy task as it requires some time, some effort, and a certain commitment. However, we also firmly believe that it can and should be a learning-journey filled with fun, moments to self-reflect, and moments of new discoveries as a new culture is explored. The final reward of speaking better English is, of course, the goal, but the journey to get to that goal should be a path of joy and smiling moments with the satisfaction of embarking on something for self-improvement.

The journey must also be a goal. After each class, you should be satisfied with making one step further to your final reward.

Becoming an 'all-rounded' and correct speaker of English requires training in not only one, but also several skills of the English language: speaking, listening, pronunciation practice, vocabulary and expression development, grammar, reading, and a little writing. In this textbook, the development of your speaking skills is strongly emphasized, but practice and training in the other important skills of communication are not neglected.

UNIT LAYOUT

The layout of each unit revolves around a grammar point or a function to help you speak correctly in a certain situation. There are 10 steps to each Unit:

STEP ONE   Objectives & Warm Up. This first step tells you clearly what you will learn in the Unit. By having a clear idea of the goals of the unit, you will be able to better focus on the skills being taught. This is followed by a pair work speaking activity in which you chat in a relaxed way with your partner in response to the questions given in the book and which are somehow related to the theme of the unit and its objectives.

STEP TWO   **Vocabulary Study.** In this step you will learn new vocabulary and expressions that will be seen in the dialogue and be given a definition of each followed by an example sentence to show how it is used. This step helps you to be more prepared to understand the dialogue.

STEP THREE   **Dialogue.** In this step you will read or listen to a dialogue about daily life in which the grammatical pattern or function is explored. This gives you the opportunity to start seeing how the grammar or function is used in a practical situation. In addition, you will learn new vocabulary and expressions that will help to further develop your communicative ability.

STEP FOUR   **Comprehension Questions on the Dialogue.** This step will help you to check and develop your understanding of the dialogue by answering questions, either in speaking or in writing, about the contents of the dialogue.

STEP FIVE   **Useful Expressions from the Dialogue.** In this step you will learn new and very useful expressions and be given a definition of each followed by an example sentence to show how it is correctly used.

STEP SIX   **Grammar Study & Speaking Practice.** In this step you will be given a clear explanation of the formation of the grammatical structure and its usage. You will be able to see how to form this grammatical or functional point, and its exact usage. You will then be given questions to practice speaking using this new grammatical or functional point.

STEP SEVEN   **Exercise Blank Fill.** This step aims to consolidate your knowledge of the grammar point by asking you to fill in the blanks of the given exercises with the correct forms based on the study points in the Unit.

STEP EIGHT   **Speaking Activity 1.** In this step you will work with a partner or subgroup to develop your speaking skills by answering questions given in the book. The questions are designed to prompt you to use the correct forms of the points being studied in the Unit.

STEP NINE **Speaking Activity 2.** In this step you will be given a speaking activity to do with your partner or subgroup in which you can demonstrate your understanding of the Unit's Objectives and apply them in an open activity. In this step the teacher can see how well you have acquired the new objectives. It is also a time for you to feel proud of your progress.

STEP TEN **Wrap Up & Guess What?** In this step there will be a reminder of when and how to use the grammatical point or function, and some advice on how to improve your speaking such as a pronunciation tip or a warning about a misused word etc. Finally, to finish off the unit on a fun note, there will be a 'Guess What?' question to see if you know the answer to some interesting facts about English or the culture. We hope that this will incite an interesting and fun discussion to finish off the Unit.

There is a famous, but very true proverb: 'The Journey of a Thousand Miles Begins with One Step'. You have made your first step through your enrolment in this course of English. Your journey has begun. Keep on the path, step by step, and enjoy the ride. Keep your eye on the final goal, but never forget to enjoy the transportation to get there. Use all the tools in each step of each unit to fix and strengthen your knowledge and create some dreams with the images we have provided to make the journey more joyful.
It has been ECK's and my great pleasure to write this book for you. As you make progress in your English development, as we are sure you undoubtedly will, your educational satisfaction, happiness, and your enhanced professional competitivity will be our honour.

ECK
Karen Dawn Ryder

Table of Contents

I WORK FOR AN INTERNATIONAL COMPANY.

UNIT 01

I work for an international company.

In this unit, you will learn how to:

- use the present simple tense in English
- speak about your daily routines/habits/schedules
- use the adverbs of frequency
- use new vocabulary and expressions about daily life

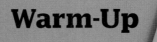

Warm-Up

Pair-work Go into pairs and discuss the following questions.

* Note: Don't worry about your accuracy. Just discuss together!

1

Q **What time do you usually wake up on a weekday? How about on the weekend?**

A

Ex. On a weekday, I usually wake up at 6 a.m. On the weekend, I usually wake up at 8 a.m.

2

Q **Do you like Mondays? Why? Why not?**

A

Ex. No, I don't like Mondays because I feel too tired after the weekend.

3

Q **What is your favorite day of the week? Why?**

A

Ex. My favorite day of the week is Friday because I can go out with my friends.

4

Q **Are you an early bird or a night owl? Why?**

A

Ex. I am an early bird because I like the quiet time of the early morning.

5

Q **Do you have a regular habit? If so, what is it?**

A

Ex. Yes. I always drink coffee in the morning when I wake up!

Vocabulary

A **Match the words with the correct meaning.**

1	line	•		•	a	a little bit, less than 'very'
2	interim agency	•		•	b	a subway route
3	local	•		•	c	near your place of work or your home
4	quite	•		•	d	a company that finds work for you
5	quiet	•		•	e	calm, relaxing
6	hectic	•		•	f	the populated area surrounding a city
7	suburbs	•		•	g	only one, unmarried
8	variety	•		•	h	very busy
9	female friends/ male friends	•		•	i	the state of having different forms or types
10	single	•		•	j	friends of the opposite or same sex but not a boyfriend/girlfriend

B **Fill in the blanks with an expression from the box.**

variety	suburbs	quite	quiet	female friends
local	single life	lines	hectic	interim agency

1 There are currently 10 subway _____ in Seoul.

2 I work for an _____ _____, so my place of work changes all the time.

3 You can enjoy a _____ of foods from different countries in Seoul.

4 I have a _____ schedule these days because it is the end of the year.

5 My house is not on a main street, so it is very _____.

6 She speaks English _____ well.

7 I prefer to live in the _____ because it is quieter and less expensive than the main city.

8 I usually eat at a _____ restaurant at lunchtime.

9 I like to have a night out with all my _____ _____ from university.

10 When I was a student, I enjoyed my _____ _____ with all my friends.

Dialogue

Two colleagues/co-workers bump into each other on the subway after not seeing each other for several months.

MP3 **01-1**

Man	Excuse me! Are you Joanna Smith who works in the Sales Department at TSM?
Woman	Oh, yes! Are you John Collins from Advertising?
Man	That's right! **Long time, no see!** How have you been?
Woman	I'm great. I moved house, so I usually take this **line** to go to work. It takes one hour on **average**.
Man	Do you still work in the Sales Department for TSM?
Woman	No, I don't. Actually, I work for an **interim agency**, so my place of work changes all the time, and I work for different companies. I like the **variety**. **How about you?**
Man	I still work for TSM. **I'm in charge of** Product Advertising, so I meet a lot of new people every day. Young people see the world differently, so we **adapt to** these changes. I have to **be on the ball**.
Woman	Do you still live in Seoul?
Man	**No way!** I don't like the **hectic** city life, so I live a **quiet** life on the weekends outside of Seoul with my dog.
Woman	Really? Where do you live?
Man	I live in the **suburbs**, in Ilsan actually. How about you?
Woman	I live in Seoul, but I want to move to the suburbs if possible. Seoul is **quite** expensive now. What do you do in your free time in the suburbs?
Man	Well, I often go for walks in the mountains with my dog. My dog loves the nature. How about you?
Woman	I go to the movies. I work out at my **local** gym and sometimes meet my **female friends**. I like my **single** life.
Man	Me too, usually. Oh, this is my stop. I get off here. Nice talking to you, Joanna! See you again!
Woman	Yes, take care. Bye!

Comprehension Check

According to the dialogue, which of the following is correct?

1 Where does this dialogue most likely take place?
   a on public transportation   b in the office   c in a pub

2 How long is the woman's commute ride on average?
   a more than one hour   b about one hour   c over one hour

3 Why does the woman like her work with the interim company?
   a She likes the company.
   b She likes her co-workers.
   c She likes doing different kinds of jobs.

4 What is the man in charge of?
   a He's in charge of Product Development.
   b He's in charge of Product Pricing.
   c He's in charge of Product Advertising.

5 The man does not live in Seoul. What are his reasons?
   a He hated the boring life of Seoul.
   b He enjoys the hectic life of the countryside.
   c He likes the laid-back life of the suburbs.

6 What does the woman want to do?
   a move to another big city   b move to a smaller town   c stay put

7 What does the man do in his free time?
   a He enjoys the company of his dog in the mountains.
   b He enjoys solitary walks in the mountains.
   c He walks dogs in the mountains.

8 What do you think is the most likely marital status of these two people?
   a They are both married.
   b They are both widowed.
   c They have no committed relationship.

9 Why does the conversation most likely end?
   a The woman arrives at her destination.
   b The train arrives at its final destination.
   c The man must disembark.

Useful Expressions

MP3 **01-2**

Let's learn the meanings and examples of the following expressions.

1	**Long time, no see!**	used as a greeting for someone you have not seen for a long time Ex. Hi, Sue! Long time, no see! It's been a year since we last met!
2	**average**	the median of an amount or figure Ex. The average grade for the exam was 85%. Some students got more, some got less. On average, how much do you spend on groceries per month?
3	**be in charge of**	be responsible for something, describe your job Ex. I am in charge of Product Design/Sales/Accounting/Marketing/ Human Resource Development/Advertising in my company.
4	**adapt to**	make changes to fit the situation Ex. Human beings can adapt to weather conditions quite well.
5	**be on the ball**	keep up to, be constantly in touch with the rapid changes that are happening Ex. We like this employee because he is always on the ball and knows exactly what the new trends are.
6	**No way!**	An informal expression used to say that you do not agree at all. A more formal way would be: 'Not at all!' Ex. A: Was the interview easy? B: No way! They asked many unexpected questions!
7	**How about you?**	used to ask the same question that was previously asked Ex. A: Do you like Seoul? B: Yes, I do. How about you? (= Do you like Seoul too?)
8	**How long does it take to...?**	used to ask about the time it takes for someone to do something or for something to be completed Ex. A: How long does it take to go to your office in the morning? B: It takes about 1 hour.

Grammar

The Present Simple

A   **Usage**   The Present Simple tense is used in English to describe our routines and usual behavior.

B   **Formation**

1 Affirmative

Subject	Verb	Object
I	speak	English.
He/She/It	speaks	English.
We	speak	English.
You	speak	English.
They	speak	English.

2 Negative

Subject	Verb	Object
I	don't speak (= do not speak)	English.
He/ She/ it	doesn't speak (= does not speak)	English.
We	don't speak (= do not speak)	English.
You	don't speak (= do not speak)	English.
They	don't speak (= do not speak)	English.

3 Interrogative

Auxiliary	Subject	Verb	Object
Do	I	speak	English?
Does	he/she/it	speak	English?
Do	we	speak	English?
Do	you	speak	English?
Do	they	speak	English?

Note We often use the simple present with the adverbs of frequency such as always, usually, often, sometimes, seldom, rarely, never.
Ex. I *always* have the same breakfast. / My friends *never* ask me about my salary because it's impolite.

C   **Practice**   Go into pairs and practice with each other.

1. What do you never do?
2. What do you always do?
3. What do you rarely do?
4. What do you sometimes do?
5. What does your boss often do?
6. Where do you seldom go?
7. What does one of your family members always do?
8. Who do you often call?
9. What do Korean people never do?
10. In which season does it usually rain in South Korea?

Exercise

A   **Fill in the blanks with the given verb in the present simple tense.**

1.   She _____ in Seoul. (live)

2.   They _____ for a major Korean company. (work)

3.   I always _____ to music in the morning. (listen)

4.   I never _____ before 6:30 a.m. (get up)

5.   My friend always _____ to work at 8:30 a.m. (go)

6.   What time _____ you usually _____ breakfast? (have)

7.   The American president _____ at the White House. (live)

8.   How often _____ your mother _____ to a sauna? (go)

9.   My pet usually _____ up before me. (wake)

10. The Earth _____ around the Sun. (rotate)

11. When _____ you usually _____ grocery shopping? (go)

12. How many times _____ you _____ _____ in a week? (work out)

13. These days the sun _____ at approximately 6 a.m. (rise)

14. The main TV news _____ at 8 p.m. (start)

15. What time _____ your boss usually _____ _____ work? (get to)

B   **Make a sentence using the prompts and the words in brackets.**

1.   I / before 6 a.m. (never wake up)

_____

2.   The newspaper / before I get up (always arrive)

_____

3.   your family / to a sauna? (ever go)

_____

4.   How often / you / your best friends? (meet)

_____

5.   What time / your office / its doors? (usually open)

_____

Speaking Activity 1

Work with a partner and answer the following questions using the simple present tense.

1 **What do you do and what are you in charge of?**

   Ex. I am a team officer for (Samsung / KT&G / Hewlett Packard) and I am in charge of Sales and Marketing.

2 **What time do you usually start and finish your job?**

   Ex. I usually start at 9 a.m. and finish at 6 p.m.

3 **How long does it take you to go to work?**

   Ex. It takes me 1 hour.

4 **What do you like to do in your free time?**

   Ex. I like to read books, and I also like to go hiking in the mountains.

5 **How often do you go to the movies?**

   Ex. I go to the movies about once a month.

6 **How often do you order food?**

   Ex. I never/rarely/sometimes/usually/always order food.

7 **How long does it take you to get ready (shower, do your hair, shave etc.) in the morning?**

   Ex. It takes me about 1 hour to get ready.

8 **Are you a night owl or an early bird? Describe your routine.**

   Ex. I am an early bird. I get up at 6 a.m. I have breakfast and respond to emails. I sometimes read the newspaper or listen to the news on television.

9 **What do you usually do to relax?**

   Ex. I like to go to a sauna, or I watch YouTube, or sometimes I listen to music.

10 **Describe the daily routine of your son or daughter, or your pet.**

   Ex. My daughter wakes up at 7 a.m. and skips breakfast. It takes her 1 hour to go to university by subway and bus. She has class every weekday and usually comes home at 8 p.m. She has dinner and then does her homework. In the evening she chats with her friends. She goes to sleep at around midnight.

Speaking Activity 2

Work with a partner.

1. Choose a famous or ordinary person or couple or group. (Example: BTS, the President, my friend, my son, my daughter)

2. Imagine their daily life and write 10 sentences to describe it. Try to make it fun and interesting.

1 _____

2 _____

3 _____

4 _____

5 _____

6 _____

7 _____

8 _____

9 _____

10 _____

3. Tell the whole class about the daily routine of your chosen person, couple, or group.

 Wrap Up & Guess What?

Remember to use the simple present tense for everyday actions.
Don't forget to put the 's' for he/she/it!

Tip   You are not a native speaker. Therefore, enunciate your words well when you speak.
Don't mumble. Speak with confidence. Like this, you can be better understood.

Guess what?

What are three things that people lose the most?

1 _____

2 _____

3 _____

UNIT 02

I'M LEAVING FOR EUROPE.

I'm leaving for Europe.

In this unit, you will learn how to:

- use the present continuous tense in English
- speak about what is happening now or the near future
- use vocabulary and expressions about daily life

Warm-Up

Pair-work Go into pairs and discuss the following questions.

*Note: Don't worry about your accuracy. Just discuss together!

1

Q **What are you doing now?**

A

Ex. Right now, I'm talking with my classmate in English.

I'm studying English.

I'm sitting at a desk and studying English with my co-workers.

2

Q **What is the teacher doing?**

A

Ex. He/she is walking around the room listening to us.

3

Q **What is the weather like right now?**

A

Ex. The sun is shining brightly.

It is raining/snowing.

The wind is blowing.

4

Q **What are you doing after this class?**

A

Ex. I'm having a meeting with my team manager.

I'm having lunch/dinner with my co-workers.

5

Q **Around what time are you going home today?**

A

Ex. I'm going home around 6 p.m.

Vocabulary

A **Match the words with the correct meaning.**

1 letdown •   • a small, not very important

2 apologize •   • b be moved to a higher and better paid position

3 slight •   • c have a deep sense of appreciation for something

4 be honored •   • d disappointment

5 fiancé/fiancée •   • e express your apology for something

6 get promoted •   • f someone to whom one is engaged to be married

7 big time •   • g the highest or most successful level, to a large extent

8 be out of town •   • h atmosphere, feeling, state of mind

9 mood •   • i beer that is served directly from the cask

10 draft beer •   • j be outside a town/city where you usually work/live

B **Fill in the blanks with the correct word and read the finished sentences out loud.**

| mood | fiancé | draft beer | apologize | are honored |
| letdown | slight | get promoted | big time | be out of town |

1 Given the expensive price, the restaurant food was a _____.

2 The sun is shining and there's a _____ breeze.

3 People are generally in a good _____ on Fridays!

4 We _____ _____ to welcome this special guest speaker.

5 Her _____ is currently doing his military service.

6 The CEO is announcing who will _____ _____ tomorrow.

7 He got into real estate _____ _____ and became a billionaire.

8 Most pubs in the U.K. serve _____ _____ rather than fancy bottled or canned beer.

9 Sorry! I'll _____ _____ _____ _____ next week. Could we schedule another time?

10 I _____ for being late. The traffic was terrible this morning!

Dialogue

Three close friends who were at university together (Jay, Joe, and Zoey), meet up for drinks at a pub after work to catch up.

* Note: Watch your pronunciation of these first names! ('J' vs 'Z')

MP3 **02-1**

Jay is already sitting in the pub when Joe comes in followed by Zoey.

Jay	*(waving)* **Over here!**
Joe	Hi Jay! Long time, no see! Zoey's just coming. She's just getting off the bus.
Jay	Oh yeah. **Here she comes**. She's just walking in. *(waving)* Over here!
Zoey	Hi. So good to see you!
Jay	What are you both drinking? **It's my treat** today! All's on me. I'm **getting promoted big time** tomorrow so I'm celebrating!
Joe	Wow! Good for you, Jay! Congratulations! A **draft beer** for me.
Zoey	**Make that two.**
Jay	So, **what's happening?** How are you doing?
Joe	Well first, I **apologize** for coughing a bit. I think I'm **coming down with** a **slight** cold. Unfortunately, I didn't get the promotion. It was a real **letdown**.
Jay	Unbelievable!
Joe	Instead, I'm moving to another company but it**'s out of town**. My wife and I are planning to move and it's taking a long time to find a new place. **On top of that,** my 8-year-old son is upset because he's leaving his elementary school friends. We're all having a hard time. But, as the song goes, 'I will survive!' How about you, Zoey?
Zoey	Oh, sorry to hear that, Joe! Well! Sorry to change the **mood** but guess what?!
Jay & Joe	What?!
Zoey	Wait for it... I'm getting married in June! We're making all the arrangements right now. In fact, I'm meeting my **fiancé** right after seeing you two. Anyway, I'm inviting you to my wedding! I would **be honored** if you both could make it.
Jay	**You bet!** That's great news, Zoey! I'm very happy for you. Sure, I'll be there!
Joe	Yes! Make that two! Congratulations! Who's the lucky man?

Comprehension Check

According to the dialogue, which of the following is correct?

1   Where is this dialogue most likely taking place?

    a at school   b at work   c in a pub

2   What is Zoey just doing?

    a She's just walking in.

    b She's ordering food.

    c She's talking on the phone.

3   Who's paying today and why?

    a Jay is paying today because he's getting promoted.

    b Joe is paying today because he's planning to move.

    c Zoey is paying today because she's getting married.

4   What are Joe and Zoey drinking?

    a red wine   b whisky   c draft beer

5   Is Joe feeling in good condition? What is his problem?

    a No, he is coming down with a slight cold.

    b Yes, he is on cloud 9.

    c No, he has chicken pox.

6   Choose one thing that Joe is looking for now.

    a a new job   b a new friend   c a new accommodation

7   How does Joe feel about his situation?

    a pessimistic   b elated   c cautiously optimistic

8   What is Zoey doing?

    a walking down the aisle

    b having a drink with her fiancé

    c planning her wedding

9   Who is she meeting after seeing Jay and Joe?

    a an acquaintance   b her relative   c her future spouse

10   When do you think they are all probably meeting next time?

    a at her wedding   b at a wedding   c at the weddings

Useful Expressions

MP3 02-2

Let's learn the meanings and examples of the following expressions.

1	**Over here!**	used to attract someone's attention in a crowded place and let them know where you are
		Ex. "Over here! A draft beer, please!" (Signalling to the server in a pub or bar)
2	**Here she/he/ it comes! Here they come!**	used to let people know that the person or thing they are waiting for is coming
		Ex. A: Wow! The food's taking a long time to arrive! B: Don't worry! Here it comes!
3	**It's my treat!**	I'm paying for this and I'm happy to do so.
		Ex. The company invited us all to a fancy restaurant this Friday and the CEO said to us, "It's my treat!"
4	**Make that two.**	an expression used to say that you want the same as the person before, or you will do the same as the person before, or you want a second one of the same thing
		Ex. A: A vanilla milkshake please. B: Oh, make that two!
5	**What's happening?**	used colloquially to ask about a person's recent news. The much more informal expression would be, "What's up?"
		Ex. Hi, John! Long time, no see. So, what's happening?
6	**come down with…**	used to express being sick with something like a fever, a cold, the flu
		Ex. I think I'm coming down with the flu that's going around.
7	**On top of that,**	to express that it is an unwelcomed addition to what you already have
		Ex. I have two reports to write. On top of that, I'm coming down with a cold.
8	**You bet!**	used to tell someone they can be sure that it will happen
		Ex. A: Are you watching the final soccer game this evening? B: You bet!

Grammar

The Present Continuous

A **Usage** The Present Continuous tense in English is used to describe actions that are happening now or are very likely to happen in the near future.

B **Formation**

1 Affirmative

Subject	To be (auxiliary)	Verb+-ing	Object
I	am	speaking	English.
He/She/It	is	speaking	English.
We	are	speaking	English.
You	are	speaking	English.
They	are	speaking	English.

2 Negative

Subject	To be (negative)	Verb+-ing	Object
I	am not (= I'm not)	speaking	English.
He/She/It	is not (= isn't)	speaking	English.
We	are not (= aren't)	speaking	English.
You	are not (= aren't)	speaking	English.
They	are not (= aren't)	speaking	English.

3 Interrogative

Auxiliary	Subject	Verb+-ing	Object
Am	I	speaking	English?
Is	he/she/it	speaking	English?
Are	we	speaking	English?
Are	they	speaking	English?

Note To make the interrogative form of this tense is easy! We just invert (switch) the subject and auxiliary (be) verb.

C **Practice** **Go into pairs and practice with each other.**

1 What are you doing now?

2 What is your teacher doing now?

3 What do you think your best friend is doing now?

4 Is it raining right now?

5 How many students are wearing navy blue in the class today?

6 What kind of watch are you wearing today?

7 Are you having dinner with your friends, family, co-workers or alone this evening?

8 What are you doing this weekend?

9 Are you enjoying yourself right now?

10 How are you feeling at the present time?

Exercise

A Fill in the blanks with the given verb in the present continuous tense.

1 My co-worker _____ _____ lunch now. (eat)

2 It's rush hour, so many Koreans _____ _____ home now. (go)

3 I think it _____ _____ now. I can hear the pitter patter of the rain. (rain)

4 What _____ you _____ after this class? (do)

5 Sorry for arriving a little late. I _____ _____ down with a cold. (come)

6 _____ anybody _____ the TV? If not, I'll turn it off. (watch)

7 Sorry. I can't make it to the restaurant. My department _____ _____
   a meeting and it _____ _____ on longer than expected. (have, go)

8 Who's _____ the meeting tomorrow? (attend)

9 Guess what! I _____ _____ promoted! (get)

10 What time _____ the train _____ tomorrow? (leave)

11 Peter! Nice to see you again! What _____ _____? (happen)

12 I'm _____ for Macau tomorrow morning on a business trip. (leave)

13 It's my treat! What _____ you _____? A draft beer? Whisky? (drink)

14 My computer _____ not _____. Could you send someone over to repair it? (work)

15 It's _____ heavily. All the main roads are blocked to the mountains. (snow)

B Make a sentence with the prompts and the words in brackets.

1 My friend / Paris / tomorrow (visit)

   _____

2 The president / a speech / right now (make or give)

   _____

3 Some co-workers / a promotion / next month (get)

   _____

4 I / the flu (come down with)

   _____

5 it / now? (rain)

   _____

Speaking Activity 1

Work with a partner and answer the following questions using the present continuous tense.

1 **What are you doing now?**

   Ex. I'm studying English.

2 **What are your co-workers or classmates doing?**

   Ex. He/she is walking around the room. / They are working at their desks.

3 **Describe the weather today using the present continuous.**

   Ex. The wind is blowing. / The sun is shining. / It is raining.

4 **What do you think your best friend is doing now?**

   Ex. I think my best friend is having a meeting.

5 **How many people are wearing black?**

   Ex. Five people are wearing black.

6 **What are you doing this weekend with your friends, family, or alone?**

   Ex. I'm having dinner with friends. / I'm visiting the in-laws. I'm binge-watching movies.

7 **Which generation do you think is having the most fun in South Korea these days?**

   Ex. I think the very young generation is enjoying life the most these days. They are not worrying about anything. They are just enjoying their life.

8 **What are you doing these days to improve your life?**

   Ex. I am trying to work out at the gym. I am trying to learn English to be a fluent speaker.

9 **What are you having for dinner this evening?**

   Ex. I think I'm having noodles or pork belly.

10 **How are you feeling now?**

   Ex. I'm feeling happy because I'm learning lots of new English words and expressions!

Speaking Activity 2

Work with a partner.

1   Imagine you are looking out the window and the scene you can see is your perfect world.

2   Discuss together what that scene is and write down 8 sentences about things that are happening in this perfect world.

Ex. Nobody is fighting. / Nobody is arguing. / Children are smiling. etc.

1   _____

2   _____

3   _____

4   _____

5   _____

6   _____

7   _____

8   _____

3   Present your sentences to the group and let us all dream together about your perfect world.

 Wrap Up & Guess What?

Remember to use the present continuous tense for actions that are happening now or for future actions that are coming soon.

Tip   Remember that the present simple (seen in Unit 01) and the present continuous (seen in this Unit) have very different usages. Therefore, try not to confuse these two tenses so that you can be clear in your English communication.

Guess what?

1   What are the names of the five fingers of the hand?

2   On what finger will Zoey and her fiancé wear their wedding ring?

THE OCTOPUS WAS MOVING WHEN IT CAME TO THE TABLE!

UNIT 03

The octopus was moving when it came to the table!

In this unit you will learn how to:

- use the simple past tense and the past continuous tense in English
- tell stories about past events
- use new vocabulary and expressions about daily life

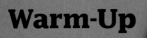

Warm-Up

Pair-work Go into pairs and discuss the following questions.

* Note: Don't worry about your accuracy. Just discuss together!

3

Q **Who did you grow up with and where did you live?**

A

Ex. I grew up with my parents, older sister, and younger brother. We lived in an old countryside house.

1

Q **Are you an early bird? What time did you get up this morning? How about last Saturday?**

A

Ex. This morning I got up at 6:30 a.m. I have to be an early bird because my work starts at 8:30 a.m. Last Saturday I got up at 9 a.m. because I had a late night out on Friday.

4

Q **What were you doing just before this class started?**

A

Ex. I was drinking a coffee. / I was sending an email to my team co-workers.

2

Q **When did you last go to a sauna? Did you enjoy it? Why? Why not?**

A

Ex. I last went to a sauna 1 month ago. I loved it! I felt very relaxed after. / I disliked it. It was far too hot. I almost passed out!

5

Q **What was the weather like yesterday?**

A

Ex. It was hot and humid. / It was very pleasant. / It was rainy. / It was warm and breezy.

Vocabulary

A   Match the words on the left with the definitions on the right.

1	fancy •	• a	twins that do not look alike in contrast to identical twins
2	raw fish •	• b	fish that is served sliced and uncooked
3	antibiotics •	• c	elegant, luxurious, very nice
4	non-identical twins •	• d	powerful drugs used to kill harmful bacteria and infections
5	cousin •	• e	(informal) a lot of
6	ugh •	• f	the child of one's uncle or aunt
7	yucky •	• g	a communicative sound to express disgust
8	loads of •	• h	a word used mainly by children to express that something does not taste good

B   Choose one of the following to fill in the blanks.

loads of	Fancy	yucky	non-identical twins
Raw fish	Ugh	cousins	antibiotics

1 _____ restaurants are usually quite expensive but not always better in taste.

2 _____ _____ should be served as fresh as possible.

3 _____! That man's touching a frog's slimy back!

4 My friend thought that it was yummy, but I thought it was _____.

5 My uncle has three children. Therefore, they are my three _____.

6 The doctor has prescribed _____ for my strong throat infection.

7 It's not hard to tell the difference between _____ _____.

8 There were _____ _____ tourists at the beach. We could hardly swim.

Dialogue

It's 9 a.m. and it's the beginning of the first morning class.
The homeroom teacher is asking how students spent their weekend.

MP3 **03-1**

Ms. Yarrow	Alright. Calm down everyone! John! Please stop **clicking** your pen and pay attention! Now, I want to hear how you all spent your weekend. Let's start with Sora.
Sora	It was my mom's birthday, so I made her a birthday card and we went to a **fancy** restaurant, but I didn't like it.
Ms. Yarrow	Why not? Why didn't you like it?
Sora	It was **raw fish** and I hate that. It was moving when it came to the table! **Ugh**!!! It was **yucky**, yucky, yucky!
Ms. Yarrow	How about you, John? And if you keep on clicking your pen, you'll get a penalty card.
John	Sorry, Ms. Yellow. I played soccer with my **cousin**, but he **sprained his ankle** while he was running so he **had to** go to the hospital.
Taemin	Yeah!!! **I bet** you kicked him just like you punched Charlie last week!
John	No, I didn't! He was trying to score a goal when he tripped up and fell!
Ms. Yarrow	Boys! Be polite. We all know that John didn't punch Charlie on purpose. And John, **be careful with** your pronunciation. My name's Yarrow, not Yellow. **Let's move on to** Gabriella. What did you do last weekend?
Gabriella	I caught a heavy cold so I couldn't go to the playground with my friends. I had to take…oh teacher you taught us the word, but I can't remember. Ah, **antibiotics**! They made me sooooo sleepy.
Ms. Yarrow	Well yes, antibiotics can make you sleepy. The last people for today are the twins Harry and Barry. They don't **look alike** but they are still twins. Can you remember what we call that?
Sora	Teacher! **Non-identical twins**.
Ms. Yarrow	That's right! So, Harry and Barry, what did you do on the weekend?
The Twins	It was our birthday, so we had a birthday party with all our friends! We got **loads of** presents, too.
Taemin	I'm your friend. Why didn't you invite me?
John	You did**n't** invite me, **either**!
Ms. Yarrow	**Let it go!** You all did a great job! Let's sing Happy Birthday to Harry and Barry.

Comprehension Check

According to the dialogue, which of the following is correct?

1   Where did this dialogue most likely take place?
    a in an office   b in a hallway   c in a classroom

2   What does John keep doing that is annoying the teacher?
    a tapping his pen   b clicking his pen   c scratching his pen

3   What does the homeroom teacher want to hear about at the beginning of class?
    a their weekend activities   b their weekend hobbies
    c their weekend studies

4   What two things did Sora do?
    a She bought a cake and went to a fancy restaurant.
    b She made a card and went to a posh restaurant.
    c She made a cake and went to a shoddy restaurant.

5   What was the raw fish doing when it came to the table and what did Sora think of it?
    a The raw fish was still moving, and she thought it was yummy.
    b The raw fish was still, and she thought it was disgusting.
    c The raw fish was still moving, and she thought it was disgusting.

6   What did John's cousin do to his ankle?
    a He sprained it.   b He broke it.   c He tortured it.

7   What did John mistakenly do to Charlie?
    a He pinched him.   b He poked him.   c He punched him.

8   Why couldn't Gabriella go to the playground?
    a She was sick.   b It was too cold.   c She caught a slight cold.

9   What are the twins' names and what kind of twins are they?
    a Their names are Harry and Barry, and they look alike.
    b Their names are Harry and Barry, and they look different.
    c Their names are Harry and Bally, and they are non-identical twins

10 What is the closest meaning of Ms. Yarrow's "Let it go!" at the end of the dialogue?
    a Stop arguing!   b Stop going there!   c Stop whispering!

Useful Expressions

Let's learn the meanings and examples of the following expressions.

1	**click**	make a short, sharp sound
		Ex. The microwave is making a strange clicking sound. Did you turn the timer off?
2	**sprain one's ankle**	twist or pull the small muscles in a joint
		Ex. Fortunately, she didn't break her wrist in the volleyball game. She just sprained her ankle.
3	**have to**	'Have to' is the same as 'must' in the present tense. It is used to make the past tense of 'must.'
		Ex. I had to chair the meeting yesterday since the team manager was absent.
4	**I bet someone did something**	guess strongly that someone did something
		Ex. I bet all the players took a long rest after such a tough match!
5	**Let's move on to…**	an expression used to transition from one idea to the next
		Ex. Let's move on to the next point on the agenda.
6	**Be careful with + noun or verb+ -ing**	advising someone to take care with something
		Ex. Be careful with the wind! / Be careful with driving!
7	**look alike**	have the same appearance
		Ex. Why is this more expensive than that? They look alike to me.
8	**not…, either**	to agree with someone's negative statement
		Ex. A: I don't like raw fish.
		B: I don't like it, either.
9	**Let it go.**	Forget about it., It's not important!
		Ex. Don't stress over a small thing. Just let it go.

Grammar 1 ▰▰▰▰▰

The Simple Past

A   **Usage** **The Simple Past tense is used to describe an event that happened in the past. We use it when we give the time that the event happened or when the time is understood by both the speaker and the listener.**

Ex.   I woke up at 6:30 a.m.
Did you watch the final soccer game?

(Note: Everybody knows that the final was aired on TV last night at 8 p.m.)

B   **Formation**

1 Affirmative

Subject	Verb	Object
I	spoke	English.
He/She/It	spoke	English.
We	spoke	English.
You	spoke	English.
They	spoke	English.

2 Negative

Subject	Verb	Object
I	didn't (= did not) speak	English.
He/She/It	didn't (= did not) speak	English.
We	didn't (= did not) speak	English.
You	didn't (= did not) speak	English.
They	didn't (= did not) speak	English.

3 Interrogative

Auxiliary	Subject	Verb	Object
Did	I	speak	English?
Did	he/she/it	speak	English?
Did	we	speak	English?
Did	you	speak	English?
Did	they	speak	English?

Note There are two types of verbs: regular and irregular. To form the past tense of the regular verbs '-ed' is added to the base verb: Ex. play → played / work → worked. However, the irregular verbs need to be memorized.

(Refer to the irregular verbs' table on page 143 and 150.)

C Practice Go into pairs and practice with each other.

1   Where did you live while you were growing up?

2   What did you eat for dinner last night?

3   Who did you last have an argument with?

4   How long did it take you to come to work/school this morning?

5   How far was your school from your home when you were a kid?

6   How many phone calls did you make yesterday? What about texts?

7   When was the last time you took a flight? Where did you fly to?

8   When did man first walk on the Moon? Who was it?

9   When did you last go to a foreign restaurant? How much was it?

10 When did you first fall in love?

Grammar 2

The Past Continuous

A **Usage** The Past Continuous tense is used to describe actions that were continuing in the past, or they were suddenly interrupted by a simple past action.

Ex. I was sleeping when you called.

A: What were you doing yesterday at 12 noon?
B: I was cleaning my home all day.

B Formation

1 Affirmative

Subject	Auxiliary	Verb	Object
I	was	speaking	English.
He/She/It	was	speaking	English.
We	were	speaking	English,
You	were	speaking	English.
They	were	speaking	English.

2 Negative

Subject	Auxiliary	Verb	Object
I	am not (= I'm not)	speaking	English.
He/She/It	is not (= isn't)	speaking	English.
We	are not (= aren't)	speaking	English.
You	are not (= aren't)	speaking	English.
They	are not (= aren't)	speaking	English.

3 Interrogative

Auxiliary	Subject	Verb	Object
Am	I	speaking	English?
Is	he/she/it	speaking	English?
Are	we	speaking	English?
Are	you	speaking	English?
Are	they	speaking	English?

Exercise

A **Fill in the blanks with an appropriate verb in the past simple or past continuous tense.**

1 We _____ raw fish and it _____ _____ when it came to the table. (order, move)

2 I _____ a cold a few days ago. (catch)

3 _____ he _____ the report on time? (submit)

4 My son _____ his ankle while he _____ _____ volleyball. (sprain, play)

5 There was a deadline, so we _____ to finish the report by midnight. (have)

6 What time _____ you _____ to be at the airport? (have)

7 I _____ _____ TV when the breaking news came on about 9/11. (watch)

8 What _____ you _____ when you heard about a terrible situation in your country? (do)

9 Last year, my brother _____ _____ from New York to San Francisco when some turbulence _____ . (fly, occur)

10 I _____ _____ to my friend when you _____ me. (talk, call)

B **Make a sentence or question with the following prompts. Use the verbs in brackets.**

1 I / ankle / while / I / play / football (break)

_____

2 Two years ago, / my friend / married (get)

_____

3 I / the subway / when / a fire (ride, break out)

_____

4 What / you / when / rain? (do, start)

_____

5 My cousin / not attention / when / the accident (pay, happen)

_____

6 The day before yesterday, the students _____ the exam. (take)

_____

7 _____ you _____ at the airport / on time? (arrive)

_____

8 When ___ you last ____ to a fancy restaurant? (go)

_____

Speaking Activity 1

Work with a partner and answer the following questions using the simple past tense or the past continuous.

1 **What did you do yesterday? Describe your day.**
Ex. Yesterday I worked all day.

2 **What were the good points and bad points of your day yesterday?**
Ex. The good point was that I did my presentation well. The bad point was that I had to work late.

3 **How many people did you meet yesterday and who were they?**
Ex. I met many people yesterday. Most were my co-workers.

4 **Describe your memories of your hometown.**
Ex. There were many old houses, and I had to walk a long way to get to school.

5 **Describe the interview that you had to get into this company.**
Ex. It was very tough. There were several interviewers, and they asked very difficult questions.

6 **When you were a child, what things did you like to do?**
Ex. We used to play games in the garden.

7 **Why did you apply to this company?**
Ex. I thought this company was one of the best and I was hoping to climb the ladder.

8 **Which person in your life influenced you the most? Why? How did they influence you?**
Ex. My grandmother influenced me the most because she always encouraged me and believed in my ability.

9 **What were you doing before you came to this company?**
Ex. I was working for a smaller company.

10 **How did you spend your university life? What kind of things did you do?**
Ex. I spent a lot of time in the library, but I also like to party with my friends.

Speaking Activity 2

Work with a partner.

1 Describe a childhood experience.

_____

_____

2 Describe a scary dream.

_____

_____

3 Describe a happy childhood experience.

_____

_____

4 Describe the first time you fell in love.

_____

_____

 Wrap Up & Guess What?

- Remember to use the simple past tense for actions in the past that refer to a specific time.
- Remember to use the past continuous for actions that were continuing in the past and were interrupted by a simple past action.

Tip It is important to know irregular verbs, so please memorize them.

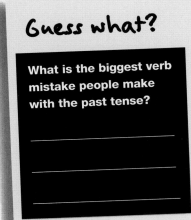

Guess what?

What is the biggest verb mistake people make with the past tense?

_____

_____

_____

This is easier than that!

In this unit you will learn how to:

- use the comparative and superlative forms of adjectives
- compare differences between things, people, places, behavior, etc.
- use new vocabulary and expressions about daily life

Warm-Up

Pair-work Go into pairs and discuss the following questions.

* Note: Don't worry about your accuracy. Just discuss together!

1

Q **What do you like more? Apple pie or ice cream? Why?**

A

Ex. I like apple pie more because it is juicier than ice cream.

2

Q **Which is more difficult for you? Getting up early or giving a presentation? Why?**

A

Ex. I'm not an early bird, so getting up early is more difficult for me.

3

Q **Who is the tallest member of your family? Who do you think is the most intelligent?**

A

Ex. My grandfather is the tallest, and I think my daughter is the most intelligent because she loves reading the 'WHY' book series.

4

Q **Which is cheaper these days? Ramen or steamed dumplings? Which do you think is better?**

A

Ex. Ramen is cheaper than dumplings, and I think steamed dumplings are better because they are healthier than ramen which is fried.

5

Q **Which actor and actress do you like most? Why?**

A

Ex. I like Leonardo Di Caprio most because he can interpret many kinds of roles.

Vocabulary

A **Match the words on the left with the definitions on the right.**

1	whereas	•	•	a	a refuge for people seeking political protection; a hospital caring for people with mental illness
2	asylum	•	•	b	an animal, plant, or person that is much smaller in size
3	populated	•	•	c	however, nevertheless
4	dwarf	•	•	d	a system in which planets rotate around a sun
5	a close game	•	•	e	inhabited, filled with people
6	solar system	•	•	f	a word to describe making a silly mistake
7	the Eiffel Tower	•	•	g	a match or a game where both teams are strong
8	Oops!	•	•	h	the most iconic tower in France

B **Fill in the blanks with a word/expression from the box.**

a close game	solar system	asylum	Oops
populated	the Eiffel Tower	whereas	dwarf

1   Gangnam and Hongdae in Seoul are highly _____ places.

2   When I visited Paris, I went to the top of _____ _____ _____.

3   I like big cities, _____ many of my friends hate crowded places.

4   Van Gogh spent time in a mental _____ where he painted many of his master pieces.

5   At half time both soccer teams were tied. It was _____ _____ _____.

6   There are 8 planets in our _____ _____.

7   Due to Pluto's size and other factors, it was rejected from our solar system and named a _____ planet.

8   _____! Sorry!

Three contestants: Suzie, Jeff, and Hugh are competing in a TV quiz show. The winner will get 100,000 dollars. The host of the quiz show is Mr. Bingo.

MP3 **04-1**

Mr. Bingo   1. Which city is more **populated**? Seoul or New York?

Suzie   Seoul!

Mr. Bingo   Correct! Seoul has approximately 10 million inhabitants. New York has 9 million.
2. Which is taller? **The Eiffel tower** in Paris or Seoul's Lotte Sky Tower?

Suzie   Lotte Sky Tower!

Mr. Bingo   Suzie's on the ball! Lotte Sky Tower is 555 meters high, **whereas** the Eiffel Tower is 330 meters. Next.
3. Who is the richest person in the world currently?

Hugh   Elon Musk!

Mr. Bingo   **You got it!** It's Elon Musk with a **net** worth of 253.2 billion US dollars. Next question:
4. This was one of Van Gogh's most famous paintings. It was called, '_____ Night.'

Jeff   *Starry Night!*

Mr. Bingo   And Jeff has got it! It was *Starry Night* which Van Gogh painted from memory while he was in the **asylum**. Next question:
5. Which is longer? The Amazon River or the Nile River?

Jeff   **I could be wrong**, but **I'll go with** the Amazon River.

Mr. Bingo   **I'm afraid** that's the wrong answer. It's the Nile. Alright it's **a close game**. Next:
6. What is the fastest animal in the world?

Suzie   **No doubt about it!** The cheetah! Its fastest speed on land is 120 km per hour.

Mr. Bingo   Dead on, Suzie! The cheetah is faster in running than all other animals. Let's keep going.
7. Which beverage has the least alcohol percentage: wine, whisky, beer, soju?

Hugh   **My instinct tells me** it's beer. I'll go with beer.

Mr. Bingo   Your instinct is correct, Hugh. It's beer. Beer is only 8% alcohol. Let's move on:
8. What is the farthest planet from the sun in our solar system?

Jeff   Pluto!

Mr. Bingo   Sorry. Pluto is not part of our **solar system** anymore. It's considered a **dwarf** planet.

Suzie   Nelly!

Mr. Bingo   **Oops!** That's not right either. Nelly is a common name for elephants.
The answer is Neptune!

Comprehension Check

According to the dialogue, which of the following is correct?

1   What are the names of the three contestants?
   a Suzie, Jeb, and Hugh   b Suzie, Jeff, and Hugh   c Suzie, Jeff, and Hug

2   According to the dialogue, which of the following is correct?
   a New York is more populated than Seoul.
   b New York is less populated than Seoul.
   c Seoul has fewer people than New York.

3   Compare Lotte Sky Tower with the Eiffel Tower in terms of height.
   a Lotte Sky Tower is steeper than the Eiffel Tower.
   b The Eiffel Tower is higher than Lotte Sky Tower.
   c The Eiffel Tower is shorter than Lotte Sky tower.

4   According to the dialogue, which is true of Elon Musk?
   a He is the wealthiest person in the world.
   b He is hardly the richest person in the world.
   c He is the least affluent person in the world.

5   What is the cheetah's fastest running speed?
   a 112 miles per hour   b 120 km per hour   c 120 miles per hour

6   Which of the following is true according to the dialogue?
   a Beer has the least alcohol percentage of the other drinks mentioned.
   b Beer has fewer calories than the other drinks mentioned.
   c The other drinks mentioned have lower alcohol percentage than beer.

7   Van Gogh's painting was called:
   a Stally Night   b Starry Light   c Starry Night

8   What is the farthest planet from the sun in our solar system?
   a Pluto   b Neptune   c Nebulous

9   Why is Suzie's answer of 'Nelly' funny?
   a Elephants are often called Nelly.
   b Elephants are never called Nelly.
   c Elephants are seldom called Nelly.

Useful Expressions

MP3 **04-2**

Let's learn the meanings and examples of the following expressions.

1	**You got it!**	an informal expression meaning 'You understand. You have understood my point.' (More formal would be 'That's right! / Absolutely! / Correct!') Ex. A: Is our meeting at 2 p.m. tomorrow? B: You got it! 2 p.m. is right.
2	**net**	the price of something after all has been deducted such as tax etc. Ex. What is my net salary?
3	**I could be wrong!**	an expression used to say that you may not have the right answer Ex. I could be wrong, but I think there are 10 million inhabitants in Seoul.
4	**I'll go with...**	I'll take... / I'll accept... Ex. A: What do you prefer? 3 p.m. or 5 p.m.? B: I'll go with 3 p.m.!
5	**I'm afraid...**	an expression used before a negative statement to make it softer Ex. A: Do you speak German? B: I'm afraid I don't, but I can understand it quite well.
6	**No doubt about it!**	It is true! Ex. A: Is Korean kimchi the best in your opinion? B: Yes, there is no doubt about it.
7	**My instinct tells me...**	I have a gut feeling. It is not logical, but I just feel something. Ex. My instinct tells me that he is the culprit. My instinct tells me that I should make a change.

Grammar

The Comparative and Superlative Forms of Adjectives

1 short adjectives

Adjective	Comparative	Superlative
big	bigger	the biggest
cheap	cheaper	the cheapest
small	smaller	the smallest

Note Adjectives ending in 'y' form the comparative with '-ier.'
Ex. easy-easier-the easiest

2 long adjectives

Adjective	Comparative	Superlative
expensive	more expensive	the most expensive
interesting	more interesting	the most interesting
comfortable	more comfortable	the most comfortable

3 special cases

Adjective	Comparative	Superlative
good	better	the best
bad	worse	the worst
little	less	the least
a lot	more	the most

Practice   Go into pairs and practice with each other.

1   What city do you prefer the most in Korea? Why?

2   Who is the most diligent person you know? Why?

3   In your opinion, what is the best way to go from Seoul to Busan? Why?

4   Is it better to be single or married? Give your reasons.

5   What is the shortest type of pasta? (spaghetti/penne/macaroni)

6   In your opinion, who is the most handsome or most beautiful actor, or actress or person you know?

7   What is the quickest way for you to go from your home to your office?

8   When you were at school, which subject was more difficult for you? Math or Social Studies?

9   What weather do you hate the most? Why?

Exercise

A **Fill in the blanks with the correct form of the adjective (comparative or superlative forms).**

1   The weather is _____ than yesterday. (mild)

2   Suzie speaks _____ English than Hugh. (good)

3   I think my bed is _____ _____ than yours. (comfortable)

4   This is the _____ test I've ever taken. (hard)

5   Today I could get a seat on the subway because there were _____ people than yesterday. (few)

6   All my friends have a lot of money. Unfortunately, I have _____ _____. (little)

7   This book is _____ than that book, so you can start out with this. (easy)

8   Which is _____ from here? Yongsan Station or Gangnam Station? (far)

9   I get up early, but my husband gets up even _____ than I do. (early)

10 Who do you like _____? New Jeans or Blackpink? (good)

11 Who do you like _____ _____? PSY? Cho Yongpil? or Na Hoon A? (good)

12 What is the _____ mountain in South Korea? (steep)

13 In your opinion, what is the _____ bug? (ugly)

14 For you, what was the _____ subject in your middle school? (easy)

15 What do you think is _____ _____? Reading a book or watching a movie? (exciting)

B **Make a sentence with the following words using a comparative or superlative form.**

1   My life is / before (easy, comparative)

   _____

2   I bought the / book / I could find (good, superlative)

   _____

3   I hope to make the / decision to maximize our company's growth.
    (profitable, superlative)

   _____

4   It was the / policy / the government has ever made (bad, superlative)

   _____

5   I ate / everybody else (a lot, comparative)

   _____

Speaking Activity 1

Work with a partner and answer the following questions using the correct form of the adjective.

1   **When is your best time of the day?**

    Ex. My best time of the day is the morning.

2   **What do you like better? Going to the movies, or going to a restaurant?**

    Ex. I like going to the movies better because I am currently on a diet!

3   **What do you think is better? The subway or the bus? Give one reason to support your opinion.**

    Ex. I think the subway is better because it is more reliable timewise.

4   **Do you like the city or the countryside better? Give one reason to support your opinion.**

    Ex. I like the city better because there are more entertainment facilities.

5   **Who makes the most delicious food in your family?**

    Ex. Actually, I think I am the one who makes the most delicious food! Maybe, my family will not agree!

6   **When are you the happiest?**

    Ex. I am the happiest on Friday evening when my work week finishes.

7   **When do you feel the loneliest?**

    Ex. I feel the loneliest when my friends do not understand me.

8   **Do you think it is better to have more free time or more money?**

    Ex. I think it is better to have more free time because if we work too much, we have less time to enjoy happy moments in life.

9   **What is the cheapest food in Korea in your opinion?**

    Ex. I think the cheapest is ramen.

10 **What is the worst time of day for you?**

    Ex. Early morning is the worst time of day for me because I am not an early bird.

Speaking Activity 2

The class should be divided into two teams: A Team and B Team.

1 The teacher gives a word to each team. For example,
A Team: Busan / B Team: Seoul.

A Team		B Team
apple		banana
i Phone	vs.	Galaxy phone
Getting married		Being single
television		the Internet

2 Each team must find an advantage for the word they are given such as
Busan is fresher than Seoul. Team B says Seoul has more educational
facilities than Busan. Other examples could be Korean National Dress
vs. Jeans and a T-shirt, or Television vs. the Internet.

_____

_____

3 The teacher will decide if the sentences are correct and give points
accordingly.

 ## Wrap Up & Guess What?

Remember the three forms of comparatives: short forms, long forms, and special
cases. Do not mix them!

Tip Be careful. Even native speakers make mistakes with
these. Don't learn English from what you hear on the
street if you want to speak correct English!

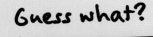

Guess what?

**What is the main
mistake people make
with the comparative
forms?**

_____

_____

_____

COULD WE HAVE THE BILL, PLEASE?

Could we have the bill, please?

In this unit you will learn how to:

- use the polite form of 'would like' instead of 'want'
- order food in a restaurant and discuss the menus
- use new vocabulary and expressions about food and restaurants

Warm-Up

Pair-work Go into pairs and discuss the following questions.

* Note: Don't worry about your accuracy. Just discuss together!

1

Q **What country's food do you like the most? Why?**

A

Ex. I like Korean food. They have many spicy dishes and I like hot food such as spicy seafood stew.

2

Q **Where do you usually eat your meals? At home? In a restaurant? From a delivery service?**

A

Ex. I usually eat breakfast at home. I eat lunch at the cafeteria, and for dinner I go out to eat.

3

Q **What is your favorite Korean dish?**

A

Ex. My favorite Korean dish is marinated beef.

4

Q **What food can you make?**

A

Ex. I can make Bolognese Spaghetti very well, and Kimchi Dumplings.

5

Q **What do you usually have for breakfast?**

A

Ex. I usually drink coffee and have yogurt with fruit.

Vocabulary

A Match the word on the left with the definition on the right.

1 actually	•	• a the main part of a western style meal usually composing of fish, meat, or seafood
2 risotto	•	• b a creamy rice dish cooked in broth
3 vinaigrette dressing	•	• c in fact; it is also used to soften a negative answer
4 main course	•	• d a French salad dressing composed of olive oil, wine vinegar, and mustard
5 dessert*	•	• e the piece of paper that shows you how much you should pay for your meal
6 bill	•	• f the last part of the meal that is sweet
7 corkage fee	•	• g a dish that we eat before the main course e.g. a salad or a soup, or other light dish
8 starter	•	• h a price you must pay if you bring your own wine to the restaurant
9 soup of the day	•	• i an expensive and hard textured seafood
10 abalone	•	• j a freshly made soup that the restaurant prepares for all the starters on that day

* Note: Be careful with the pronunciation. The stress is on the second syllable.

B Fill in the blanks with a word/expression from the box.

starter	Abalone	Vinaigrette dressing	corkage fee	bill
Actually	dessert	soup of the day	main courses	risotto

1 I don't like foie gras. _____, I hate it.

2 I took the green salad for the _____.

3 _____ _____ is the most widely used dressing in France.

4 All the _____ _____ are usually served with vegetables.

5 Today's _____ ___ _____ _____ is 'Broccoli and Bacon Cream' soup.

6 _____ porridge is very popular in South Korea.

7 Mushroom _____ is a popular dish in Italy.

8 The _____ _____ is $10 per bottle.

9 Apple pie or ice cream is a favorite _____ for children!

10 It's always a good idea to check the _____ to avoid mistakes.

Dialogue

Three graduate students (Kay, Gina, and Scott) go out for dinner in a trendy restaurant in New York.

MP3 **05-1**

Kay	**I'm starving**! Let's go in here. It's an Italian restaurant, but it's popular and so you**'re supposed to** make a reservation first so we might **be out of luck**...
Scott	Looks great! **What d'ya think**, Gina**?**
Gina	Fine by me! I've missed Italian food very much since my family and I moved back to the USA **after living** in Rome for 2 years.

(They go into the restaurant and the waiter greets them.)

Kay	A table for three, please.
Waiter	Do you have a reservation?
Kay	**Actually**, no. We've just come **on the off chance**.
Waiter	You are in luck. We've just had a **last-minute** cancellation. Right this way, please.

(They look at the menu and choose. The waiter comes over to take their order.)

Gina	I'd like the Mixed Salad for the **starter** with **vinaigrette dressing** and the Bolognese Spaghetti for the **main course**.
Kay	I'll take the **Soup of the Day** and then **Abalone Risotto** for the main.
Scott	I'll skip the starter, but I'd like the Gorgonzola Pizza for the main, and can you **go light on** the garlic?
Waiter	Sure. And to drink?
Scott	Oh, we've brought our own wine. What is the **corkage fee**?
Waiter	You're in luck again. This evening is corkage-free night.

*(They finish the meal after the **dessert**.)*

Kay	Excuse me. Can we have the **bill** please?

(Kay looks at the bill with the intention to pay all but with shock.)

Kay	D'ya mind if we **go Dutch**?
Gina	No, don't worry, I've got it!
Scott	I've got my parents' credit card here. Don't worry about it. **It's** all **on me!** Or my parents!

Comprehension Check

According to the dialogue, which of the following is correct?

1   Why is Kay worried about this restaurant?

    a The restaurant has a poor reputation

    b The food might not be good.   c They didn't make a reservation.

2   Why does Gina really want to go to this Italian restaurant?

    a She is longing for Italian food again.   b She is starving.

    c She has never been to Italy and want to try Italian food.

3   Did they make a reservation to go to this restaurant?

    a No, but they are trying their luck.

    b Yes, but they are still worried about getting a table.

    c No, so they are going to another Italian restaurant.

4   Why were they able to get a table?

    a The restaurant was almost empty.

    b They waited for ages until a table became free

    c A reservation was suddenly broken.

5   What exactly does Scott say to mean that he will not take a starter?

    a I'll scan the starter.   b I'll scrape the starter.   c I'll skip the starter.

6   How does Scott feel about garlic?

    a He can't stand it.   b He can't get enough of it.

    c He likes it in moderation.

7   What did they not have to pay for?

    a the opening of their own wine and the wine glasses

    b the valet parking   c waitress service

8   What did Kay want to do regarding payment?

    a treat everyone   b pay just for her own food

    c pay for the starters only

9   Who initially wanted to pay for everyone until she saw the bill?

    a Scott   b Gina   c Kay

10   Who really pays in the end?

    a Scott's parents   b Scott's in-laws   c Scott's siblings

Useful Expressions

MP3 05-2

Let's learn the meanings and examples of the following expressions.

1	**be starving**	be very hungry. Ex. I'm starving. I haven't eaten all day!
2	**be supposed to…**	be expected to do something Ex. Younger people are supposed to give their seats to the elderly on the subway.
3	**be out of luck**	have an unfavorable situation Ex. All the tickets were already sold, so I was out of luck.
4	**What d'ya think?**	an informal way of speaking to say, 'What do you think?' Ex. Hey, man! What d'ya think?
5	**after + V-ing**	after doing something Ex. After taking a nap, I felt much more energetic.
6	**on the off chance**	the slight possibility that something can happen Ex. I went to the airport on the off chance there would be a no show and I could get a seat.
7	**last-minute**	done or occurring at the latest possible time before an event or very close to a deadline Ex. He made some last-minute changes to his homework.
8	**go light on…**	reduce something Ex. Please go light on the salt and sugar!
9	**go Dutch**	share the cost of something, especially a meal, equally Ex. Most students usually go Dutch when they pay for their food in a restaurant.
10	**It's on me!**	I will pay for this! Ex. Eat what you want! It's all on me!

Grammar

The polite usage of 'would like'

A **Usage** **The usage of 'want' has three styles in English. You should fit the style to suit the situation.**

1 **formal style: would like (being very polite to someone)**

Ex. A: What would you like to order?
     B: I'd like the house specialty, please.

2 **standard style: want (speaking in every day style)**

Ex. A: What do you want to order?
     B: I want the soup of the day.

3 **informal style: wanna (with your close friends. speaking very casually)**

Ex. What d'ya wanna order?

Note We can use would like, want, and wanna with the full infinitive or a noun.

Ex. I would like to go.

   I want to go.

   I wanna go.

   I would like a coffee.

   I want a coffee.

   I wanna coffee.

Exercise

A   **Fill in the blanks with an appropriate phrase that you learned from the dialogue. Some words are given in brackets to help you.**

1   I _____ starving! (be)

2   You _____ _____ to make a reservation. However, you could be lucky. (be supposed)

3   I _____ Korean food. I haven't eaten it for a long time. (miss)

4   I know we don't have a reservation, but let's go on the _____ _____ there will be a free table. (chance)

5   We are in luck! There was a _____ cancellation! (minute)

6   Could you _____ _____ on the salt? I'm trying to cut down! (light)

7   What is the _____ _____? We have brought our own wine. (fee)

8   We'd like to pay. Could we _____ the _____, please? (bill)

9   When I was at university, my friends and I always _____ _____ when we went to a restaurant because we were all on a budget. (Dutch)

10   I always take the three courses in a meal: _____, _____ _____, and then the _____.

B   **Imagine you are in a restaurant. Make a sentence or question with the following words.**

1   I / the chicken salad (order)

_____

2   I'd like the curry, but could you _____ _____ on the spices? (light)

_____

3   We've brought our own wine. What is the _____ _____? (fee)

_____

4   How _____ you _____ your steak? Rare, medium, or well-done? (like)

_____

5   _____ we _____ the _____, please? We are ready to leave. (bill)

_____

Speaking Activity 1

Work with a partner and answer the following questions about restaurants and eating out.

1 How often do you go out to eat with your family?

Ex. I go out to eat once a week.

2 What kind of restaurant do you like to go to?

Ex. I usually go to an Italian or a Korean restaurant.

3 Do you make a reservation, or do you go on the off chance?

Ex. I usually go on the off chance.

4 What is your favorite type of dressing? Why?

Ex. I like vinaigrette because it is a little oily but also tangy.

5 If you eat meat, how do you like your meat to be cooked? (rare, medium, or well-done)

Ex. I like it medium to well-done because I don't like to see red meat.

6 What is your favorite type of dessert? (light or heavy ones)

Ex. I like heavy desserts even though they are not good for health.

7 Tell your partner or group about your favorite restaurant and why you like it.

Ex. My favorite restaurant is called Mom's Kitchen. I like it because it is reasonably priced, and the quality and service are very good.

8 Have you ever been overcharged?

Ex. I was once overcharged in a foreign country.

9 What are the good points and bad points of Korean food?

Ex. Korean food is very healthy because it has many vegetables. However, it is sometimes too salty or spicy.

10 What is your opinion of fast food?

Ex. Fast food is sometimes convenient when we are in a hurry, or we have a tight budget. Nevertheless, it is bad for health due to its high salt and sugar content.

Speaking Activity 2

Work with a partner.

1 Choose a dish that you both like (either Korean or Western) and give 3 reasons why you recommend going to that place where they serve that dish, or why you recommend that dish.

1 _____

_____

2 _____

_____

3 _____

_____

 Wrap Up & Guess What?

Remember to use 'would like + noun' or 'would like to + verb' when ordering food in a polite way.

Tip It takes time to appreciate another country's food. Give it a chance. I, as a foreigner, hated Korean food when I came here. Now I love it. I love kimchi more than Koreans do! Give it a chance.

Guess what?

What are the most famous dishes in Korea for foreigners?

1 _____

2 _____

3 _____

I HAVEN'T FOUND THE RIGHT PERSON YET!

UNIT 06

I haven't found the right person yet!

In this unit you will learn how to:

- use the present perfect simple tense in English
- speak about your life experiences so far without giving a specific time
- use new vocabulary and expressions about daily life

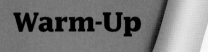

Warm-Up

Pair-work Go into pairs and discuss the following questions.

* Note: Don't worry about your accuracy. Just discuss together!

1

Q **How many foreign countries have you visited?**

A

Ex. I have visited three foreign countries. / I have never been abroad.

2

Q **Have you ever eaten strange foreign food? If so, what was it? Can you describe it?**

A

Ex. Yes, I have. I have eaten 'snails' cooked in garlic. They were very rubbery and not delicious in my opinion.

3

Q **Have you ever been bungee jumping? Describe your experience.**

A

Ex. No, I haven't. I think it's crazy. / Yes, I have. It's very thrilling.

4

Q **What have you just done?**

A

Ex. I have just answered your question. / I have just finished lunch.

5

Q **Who have you already called today?**

A

Ex. I have already called my boss, and my father-in-law.

Vocabulary

A   Match the words on the left with the definitions on the right.

1	retired	a	holding traditional values
2	bucket list	b	having left one's job
3	conservative	c	things that a person wants to do before he/she dies
4	abide by	d	beyond a reasonable amount
5	excessive	e	the extra parts of a western meal such as the potatoes, the vegetables, the sauce etc.
6	the trimmings	f	accept or obey an agreement or rule
7	beloved	g	a person who has retired and receiving a pension from the government
8	pensioner	h	a foolish person, a person of low intelligence
9	lunatic	i	a crazy person
10	moron	j	dearly loved

B   Fill in the blanks with an expression from the box.

conservative	abide by	lunatic	excessive	bucket list
pensioners	retired	moron	beloved	the trimmings

1   For the safety of all, we should _____ _____ the driving traffic rules.

2   Who was that _____ who left the house door open?

3   The political right wing usually holds _____ viewpoints.

4   He _____ at the age of 65.

5   These days, many _____ enjoy an active lifestyle.

6   It was stupid of me to say that; I acted like a complete _____.

7   After his death, she mourned her _____ husband for years.

8   Food prices these days are _____.

9   The turkey Christmas lunch was served with all _____ _____.

10 Visiting the Taj Mahal is on my _____ _____.

Interview

Mr. Ralph Riggins is one of the few people in England who are over 100 years old. Yesterday, a TV reporter came to his house to ask him about his life so far.

MP3 06-1

Interviewer (or TV reporter) What are your secrets for a long life?

Mr. Riggins Well, I've never thought about that question, but **come to think of it** now, my lifestyle might have helped.

Interviewer How so?

Mr. Riggins I have had a few simple rules that I've mostly **abided by** my whole life. The first is that I have never listened to those **morons** who tell me how to live my life such as what to wear, and how to behave. I've always done what feels good **providing** it does no harm to others.

Interviewer It sounds great!

Mr. Riggins Look at the clothes I'm wearing today, for instance! I'm in a pair of ripped jeans, and a T-shirt even though many idiots say these clothes are only for youngsters. Do I look good, **or what!?** (Hahaha)

Interviewer You look great!

Mr. Riggins In fact, I've always worn jeans except for formal occasions like weddings and funerals. Those same **lunatics** sometimes say that seniors should be **conservative** in their political opinions, but I've never believed in something just because I'm a **retired pensioner**. I've always thought deeply about social and political issues and voted **according to** my beliefs, not according to my age.

Interviewer More people should follow that advice!

Mr. Riggins Right! Secondly, I've never listened to all those lunatics who say that you should **give up** all **the pleasures of life**! Don't eat this! Don't eat that! I've never listened to them. I like **the joys of life**. Although I've never drunk alcohol **excessively**; I have always drunk a few glasses of good wine with every evening meal. For example, I've just had a roast pork dinner with all **the trimmings** with my tennis club friends, and a couple of glasses of champagne, three, because I'm the **birthday boy** today and they treated me to all!

Interviewer Congrats!

Mr. Riggins I've always enjoyed everything **in moderation**. Ah! **Believe it or not**, there are still many things that I haven't done yet.

Interviewer Really? What are they?

Mr. Riggins One of them is to go on the national song contest on TV and sing 'Fly Me to the Moon'! The second is to **tie the knot** again! My **beloved** wife passed away 10 years ago, but I've felt a bit lonely the last few years. I haven't found the right lady yet. So… If there is anybody out there watching this who is the same age as me or a bit older or younger, then let's give it a go. Let's enjoy our **bucket list** together! My last piece of advice that I have always remembered is that '**Age is Just a Number**'. **You are only as old as you feel!**

Comprehension Check

According to the dialogue, which of the following is correct?

1   Why is Mr. Riggins a remarkable man?

   a Even though he is middle-aged, he is very active.

   b Even though he is in the prime of life, he is very active.

   c Even though he is in the winter of his life, he is very active.

2   Why did the TV reporter visit his home?

   a to get advice on how to live a long life

   b to find out about his personal life

   c to tell him some secrets

3   What is Mr. Riggins' first rule?

   a He always listens to people who give him advice on how to live his life.

   b He refuses to listen to people who give him advice on how to live his life.

   c He treats everyone as a moron.

4   So far, when has he never worn jeans and a T-shirt?

   a to go shopping   b to go biking   c to weddings and funerals

5   What has he always done in relation to political and social ideas?

   a He has considered them carefully.

   b He has considered them lightly.

   c He hasn't given them deep thought.

6   What has he always done with regards to wine?

   a He has never touched it.

   b He drinks a couple of glasses as a nightcap.

   c He drinks a couple of glasses while dining.

7   What is the first thing he hasn't done yet?

   a He hasn't sung 'Fly Me to the Moon' yet.

   b He hasn't participated in the country's National Song Contest yet.

   c He hasn't flown to the moon yet.

8   What is the last thing he hasn't found yet?

   a a new sport   b a new sponsor   c a new spouse

9   What is Mr. Riggins' opinion about age?

   a It's just a fraction.   b It's just a number.   c It's just a percentage.

10 What do we call a person who is 100 years old or older?

   a a century   b a centipede   c a centenarian

Useful Expressions

Let's learn the meanings and examples of the following expressions.

1	**Come to think of it!**	Now that it suddenly comes to my mind! Ex. Oh! Come to think of it! I think the meeting has been postponed. Could you check?
2	**Providing…**	On condition that… Ex. Providing the weather is good, the flight will take off on time.
3	**…or what?**	an expression to show exaggeration or give emphasis Ex. Wow! Is it snowing or what?! Wow! Is he handsome or what?!
4	**, and the like**	and other similar things to the ones just mentioned. Ex. My parents like to go hiking, walking, canoeing, and the like.
5	**according to…**	following what this person or this article said Ex. According to the weather forecast, it will be a sunny and pleasant day tomorrow.
6	**the pleasures/ joys of life**	the good things that we can enjoy in our life Ex. According to Mr. Riggins, we should remember to enjoy the pleasures of life such as good food, alcohol in moderation, spending some money on ourselves, or for others etc.
7	**the birthday boy/girl**	the person who has a birthday on that day Ex. Let's sing Happy Birthday to the birthday girl!
8	**give up**	stop something or doing something Ex. Due to health reasons, many people have given up their smoking habits or junk food.

9	**Believe it or not,**	an expression used before announcing something that your listener might not believe
		Ex. Believe it or not, it's going to be even hotter tomorrow!
10	**Age is just a number. / You are only as old as you feel.**	Two expressions to say that age is not a factor to determine your lifestyle, health, or outlook on life.
		Ex. Many older people lead active and very healthy lifestyles these days which proves that age is just a number.
11	**tie the knot**	get married
		Ex. My parents tied the knot after dating for two years.
12	**in moderation**	within reasonable limits; not to excess
		Ex. All things are good for us, in moderation!

Grammar

The Present Perfect

A Usage The Present Perfect tense (has/have p.p.) is used in English to describe your experiences without giving a precise time or used with the words **ever, never, just, already, not...yet, since, for.**

B Formation

1 Affirmative

Subject	Auxiliary	Verb	Object
I	have	seen	the movie.
He/She/It	has	seen	the movie.
We	have	seen	the movie.
You	have	seen	the movie.
They	have	seen	the movie.

2 Negative

Subject	Auxiliary	Verb	Object
I	have not (= haven't)	seen	the movie.
He/She/It	has not (= hasn't)	seen	the movie.
We	have not (= haven't)	seen	the movie.
You	have not (= haven't)	seen	the movie.
They	have not (= haven't)	seen	the movie.

3 Interrogative

Auxiliary	Subject	Verb	Object
Have	I	seen	the movie?
Has	he/she/it	seen	the movie?
Have	we	seen	the movie?
Have	you	seen	the movie?
Have	they	seen	the movie?

Exercise

A   Fill in the blanks with an appropriate verb form.

Irregular verbs

infinitive	past simple	past participle	infinitive	past simple	past participle
1 be	was / were		36 keep		
2 become			37 know		
3 begin			38 learn		
4 break			39 leave		
5 bring			40 lend		
6 build			41 let		
7 burn			42 lose		
8 buy			43 make		
9 catch			44 meet		
10 choose			45 pay		
11 come			46 put		
12 cost			47 read		
13 cut			48 ride		
14 do			49 run		
15 draw			50 say		
16 dream			51 see		
17 drink			52 sell		
18 drive			53 send		
19 eat			54 shut		
20 fall			55 sing		
21 feed			56 sit		
22 feel			57 sleep		
23 find			58 speak		
24 fly			59 spend		
25 forget			60 swim		
26 freeze			61 swing		
27 get			62 take		
28 give			63 teach		
29 go			64 tell		
30 grow			65 think		
31 have			66 throw		
32 hear			67 wake		
33 hit			68 wear		
34 hold			69 win		
35 hurt			70 write		

* Note: It is important to memorize the formation of these verbs. Check with your teacher for the correct forms.

B **Make a sentence or a question with the following words. Use the present perfect tense.**

1   I / already / the movie (see)

_____

2   My friend / just / the USA (go)

_____

3   I / lunch / yet (not have)

_____

4   You / ever / to a French restaurant? (be)

_____

5   My parents / never / a presentation (give)

_____

6   How many times / a sauna / in your life so far? (visit)

_____

7   Most people / never / their first love (forget)

_____

8   How long / you / in this country? (live)

_____

9   What / you / already / today? (eat)

_____

10 What / you / never / in your life so far? (do)

_____

Speaking Activity 1

Work with a partner and answer the following questions about your experiences.

1 ## How many times have you been abroad in your life so far?

Ex. I have been abroad 5 times so far.

2 ## Have you ever been camping? How many times?

Ex. Yes, I have. I have been camping about 8 times.

3 ## What have you not done yet today?

Ex. I haven't paid my electricity bills so far today.

4 ## What have you already done today?

Ex. I have already scheduled three meetings for next week with my teammates.

5 ## How long have you worked in this company?

Ex. I have worked in this company for 8 years.

6 ## How long have you lived in your present place?

Ex. I have lived here/there for 2 years.

7 ## Who have you just spoken to?

Ex. I have just spoken to my English classmate.

8 ## Have you ever been sick after a restaurant?

Ex. Yes, I have. It was because of oysters which I ate in summer.

9 ## What things have just happened in your office?
Ex. We have just finished a meeting.

10 ## How long have you been in your office today?

Ex. I have been in my office since this early morning. I will soon go home.

Speaking Activity 2

Work with a partner.

1   Tell your partner about your 'secrets' for a long life. Tell your partner what you have always done and why. Remember to try to use the present perfect. Give your secrets for a long and happy life.

_____

_____

_____

_____

_____

 ## Wrap Up & Guess What?

Remember to use 'have/has p.p.' for actions that have no specific time indication, and when you use the words: ever(?), never, just, already, not…yet, since, and for.

Tip Please note that many American speakers do not use this present perfect tense as much as the British or Europeans or Australian speakers if the meaning is clear by the context. However, if you are planning to take a test, then you had better know the difference.

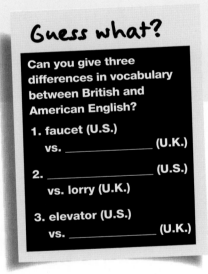

Guess what?

Can you give three differences in vocabulary between British and American English?

1. faucet (U.S.)
   vs. _____ (U.K.)

2. _____ (U.S.)
   vs. lorry (U.K.)

3. elevator (U.S.)
   vs. _____ (U.K.)

WHY DON'T YOU TALK TO YOUR BOSS ABOUT IT?

Why don't you talk to your boss about it?

In this unit you will learn how to:

- make suggestions and give advice
- use the patterns of 'Why don't you do...?', 'How about doing...?', 'If I were you, I would...'
- use new vocabulary and expressions about daily life

Warm-Up

Pair-work Go into pairs and discuss the following questions.

* Note: Don't worry about your accuracy. Just discuss together!

1

Q **Do you like to receive advice from others?**

A

Ex. No, I usually make decisions on my own. / Yes, I like to hear my friends' opinions.

3

Q **How often do you give advice to your friends or your colleagues?**

A

Ex. I only give advice to my colleagues if they ask for it.

2

Q **Whose advice do you respect the most?**

A

Ex. I always listen to my closest friends' advice.

5

Q **What is the advice that you remember most from your parents?**

A

Ex. My mother always told me to do everything in moderation.

4

Q **Do you follow the advice you receive?**

A

Ex. Mostly I just listen, but I do not follow their advice.

Vocabulary

A **Match the word on the left with the definition on the right.**

1	hectic	•	• a	an employee in a company who has the power to put plans and actions into effect
2	upturn	•	• b	the amount of money coming in
3	revenue	•	• c	an increase, an improvement in trend
4	executive	•	• d	very busy
5	hardship	•	• e	a rank in a company that superior to yours
6	C'mon!	•	• f	feel the effects of stress
7	downturn	•	• g	a difficult period
8	tighten the belt	•	• h	a decrease, a decline in trend
9	stress out	•	• i	Come on! (an informal expression to encourage, or doubt someone)
10	higher up	•	• j	cut down on expenses

B **Fill in the blanks with an expression from the box.**

revenue	hardship	C'mon	executive	tighten the belt
hectic	higher-up	upturn	downturn	stress out

1   It was a _____ schedule this morning.

2   There was an _____ in sales last month.

3   The _____ of small businesses was low this quarter.

4   Some companies are losing money, due to the economic _____.

5   There was much _____ during the I.M.F. period.

6   _____! You can do it!

7   The sales _____ decided to launch the new product.

8   The family of four needed to _____ _____ _____ in the I.M.F. period.

9   Try not to _____ _____ too much!

10   We sometimes disagree with the _____ policies.

Dialogue

Two close colleagues meet up for dinner and drinks after work on Friday. They pour out their problems to each other.

Kevin   So, it's been quite a **hectic** week, right!?

Johnny   **No kidding!** My boss has **been on my back** all week.
I've done my best, but my best is not good enough in his eyes.
Profits are down and I'm responsible for making an **upturn**. I'm not sure
how I can **make it happen**.

Kevin   **Why don't you** sit down and have a talk with him about it**?**

Johnny   **Easier said than done!**

Kevin   Then **how about** inviting him for a relaxed lunch and...

Johnny   **No way!** He's **as busy as a bee** every single day. **Come to think of it,**
I've never seen him take a break. He**'s** always **on the go**!
I've gotta increase sales **revenue** by the end of this quarter otherwise
my job is on the line.

Kevin   Hey, **c'mon** Johnny. You are one of the best sales **executives** in this company.
If I were you, I would just tell the boss that you need a bit of time
in this economic **downturn**. All companies are going through
hardship these days and are **tightening the belt**. In my opinion,
he's just **stressing out** too from the pressure from **higher up**.
We**'re** all **in the same boat. Chin up!** My story is worse than yours.

Johnny   Oh yeah? Tell me about it...

Comprehension Check

According to the dialogue, which of the following is correct?

1   What kind of a week has Johnny had?
   a laid back
   b very busy
   c moderate

2   Why has Johnny's week been terrible?
   a He's back at work after a holiday.
   b His boss has been giving him a hard time.
   c Johnny doesn't feel well enough.

3   How does Kevin make his suggestion?
   a Why do you talk with your boss?
   b Why don't you talk with your boss?
   c Why would you talk with your boss?

4   Why do you think Johnny says, "Easier said than done."
   a Because speaking with his boss is easy.
   b Because speaking with his boss is not so hard.
   c Because it's easy to say that, but not easy to carry it out.

5   What might happen to Johnny if sales do not increase?
   a He may lose his job.
   b He will keep his job.
   c He must change his job.

6   How did Kevin describe Johnny?
   a You are the one and only best sales executive in the company.
   b You can be one of the best sales executives in the company.
   c You and a few others are the best sales executives in the company.

7   What is Kevin's last piece of advice? What exactly does he say?
   a If I were you, I would tell the boss…
   b If I were you, I would told the boss…
   c If I were you, I would telling the boss…

Useful Expressions

MP3 07-2

Let's learn the meanings and examples of the following expressions.

1	**No kidding.**	I am serious. Ex. Salaries are going up next year. No kidding. It was an official announcement in the meeting.
2	**be on someone's back**	bother someone in a negative way Ex. My boss has been on my back all week.
3	**make something happen**	put a plan into action Ex. The President has the power to make it happen!
4	**Easier said than done!**	an expression used to say that it is not easy at all to do Ex. The rules to lose weight are easier said than done!
5	**No way!**	(informal) Not at all! Ex. A: Can we start class tomorrow at 6 a.m.? 　　B: No way!
6	**as busy as a bee**	(simile) very busy Ex. I'm as busy as a bee all week!
7	**come to think of it, …**	suddenly realize Ex. Oh sorry. Come to think of it, I can't meet tomorrow at 7 p.m. I have a company dinner!
8	**be on the go**	be moving around a lot, be very busy Ex. I am very busy. I'm on the go all week.
9	**be in the same boat**	experience the same things (usually negative) Ex. Your life is hectic. My life is hectic. We are in the same boat!
10	**Chin up!**	Try to stay positive! Ex. Chin up! It won't last forever!

Grammar

How to Make Suggestions or Give Advice

Let us look at some ways to make suggestions or give advice to someone in English.

1 How about + verb + -ing / noun?

> Ex. How about taking an aspirin?
> How about a double espresso to wake you up?

2 Why don't you + do?

> Ex. Why don't you talk to your boss about this problem?
> Why don't you ask for a pay raise?

3 You'd(= You had) better + do

> Ex. You'd better take a taxi, otherwise you will be late for the meeting.
> We'd better skip dessert because our meeting starts in 5 minutes.

4 If I were you, I would(= I'd) + do

> Ex. If I were you, I would talk to my boss about the problem.
> What would you do if you were me?

5 Let's + do (if you are included in the suggestion)

> Ex. If it's okay with you, let's meet at 6 p.m.
> Let's have an end of year party to boost morale!

6 I think you should + do

> Ex. I think you should take a vacation to get some rest.
> I think our team should continue with this project.

7 It would/might be a good idea to + do

> Ex. It would be a good idea to make a kakao business channel to advertise our products.
> It might be a good idea to take your umbrella today; heavy rain is forecast.

8 Have you thought about + verb + -ing?

> Ex. Have you thought about selling some of things on e-bay?
> Have you thought about changing jobs?

Exercise

A **Fill in the blanks with an appropriate verb in the correct form.**

1   How about _____ for a raise? (ask)

2   How about _____ _____ earlier to avoid the traffic jam? (get up)

3   Why don't you _____ for a raise? (ask)

4   If you want to lose weight, how about _____ to work? (walk)

5   If I were you, I would _____ the boss for a raise. (ask)

6   You'd better _____ a taxi if you want to arrive on time! (take)

7   If you agree, let's _____ at 8 p.m. in Gangnam! (meet)

8   I think you should _____ at a more convenient time. (call)

9   Have you thought about _____ a cheaper hotel? (book)

10 Let's _____ home and watch a movie this weekend. (stay)

11 How about _____ the short cut? (take)

12 Why don't your children _____ a school nearer to your home? (attend)

13 Have you thought about _____ a deposit to reserve the hotel room? (send)

14 The exam is tomorrow! He'd better _____ hard this evening to prepare for the test. (study)

15 Let's _____ the next exercise. (do)

B **Read the following, and then be prepared to give your advice for each situation.**

1   John never studies because he likes watching YouTube until late in the evening.

    Your advice: _____

    _____

2   It's snowing heavily and your friend has a very bad back.

    Your advice: _____

    _____

3   Your subordinate always arrives late for work.

Your advice:

_____

_____

4   You know your best friend is unhappy with his girlfriend and you saw her cheating with another man.

Your advice:

_____

_____

5   Your best friend hates the summer weather and can hardly function in the summer weather.

Your advice:

_____

_____

6   Your colleague is having some chest pains.

Your advice:

_____

_____

7   Your friend can't stand waiting for buses that are always crowded in Seoul.

Your advice:

_____

_____

8   Your friend has financial problems but drives an expensive car and eats expensive food.

Your advice:

_____

_____

9   Your sister cannot sleep at night. She drinks several cups of coffee per day.

Your advice:

_____

_____

Speaking Activity

1 Think of some problems you have recently. It could be at work, in your home,
in your commute ride etc. Take some notes to remember your problem.
Then, go into pairs or groups of three.
Each person should tell the other/others the problem.
After listening, give your classmate some advice or make a suggestion.

Ex.

Student A My son plays too many video games in the evening and so his school grades are
going down.

Student B How about using an app to block video games during the week and allowing them
only on Friday nights?

_____

_____

_____

_____

_____

2 At the end of this activity, each person should say if they received good
advice and if they will follow it.

 Wrap Up & Guess What?

Remember how to give advice to someone in English:

1 Why don't you...?
2 How about doing...?
3 If I were you I would...
4 You had better...
5 Let's...
6 I think you should...
7 It would/might be a good idea to...
8 Have you thought about...?

Guess what?

What topics of advice do
many moms want when
they visit a palm reader?
How about young people
who are going to graduate?
How about dads?

1 _____

2 _____

3 _____

UNIT 08

EXCUSE ME!

COULD YOU
TELL ME

HOW TO
GET TO
THE
STATION?

Excuse me! Could you tell me how to get to the station?

In this unit you will learn how to:

- use the imperative form in English
- give and politely ask for directions
- use new vocabulary and expressions about daily life

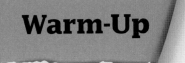

Warm-Up

Pair-work Go into pairs and discuss the following questions.

* Note: Don't worry about your accuracy. Just discuss together!

1

Q **Do you have a good sense of direction?**

A

Ex. Yes, I think so because I rarely get lost. / No, I'm hopeless at finding my way.

2

Q **Do you like to ask people for directions, or do you prefer to figure it out yourself?**

A

Ex. I usually try to figure it out, but if I fail after five minutes, I ask someone for help.

3

Q **Have you ever asked someone if they needed help?**

A

Ex. Yes. I once helped a foreigner on the street who was struggling to find the way.

4

Q **Do you think the city/ town where you live is easy to navigate?**

A

Ex. I live in Seoul, and I think the signs and subway system are easy to follow.

5

Q **How do you get to your place of work?**

A

Ex. I take the subway from Yongsan Station. I transfer one time to go to Gangnam.

Vocabulary

A   **Match the word on the left with the definition on the right.**

1	block •	• a	the intersection between two or more roads
2	crossroads •	• b	put into a position
3	bill •	• c	place, fit or push into something else
4	place •	• d	the paper form of money
5	select •	• e	the distance on a street between the roads that intersect it
6	insert •	• f	visit someone unexpectedly for a short visit
7	recharge •	• g	choose
8	drop by •	• h	give new energy (electrical, physical) to something/someone
9	otherwise •	• i	requiring immediate attention
10	urgent •	• j	if the conditions are not met

B   **Fill in the blanks with a word from the box.**

insert	blocks	selected	placed	dropped by
bill	recharge	otherwise	urgent	crossroads

1   My apartment is only two _____ from the nearest subway station.

2   There are no traffic lights at this small _____, so drive carefully.

3   I need to _____ my cell phone.

4   Artworks need to be correctly _____ in a museum for maximum effect.

5   We _____ the best room for the conference.

6   Please _____ your card into the slot.

7   The most basic form of U.S. paper currency is the one-dollar _____.

8   I didn't call in advance, I just _____ _____.

9   I must pay my electric bill, _____ it will be cut off!

10   The CEO suddenly announced an _____ meeting.

Dialogues

The following are three situations in which the imperative forms are used to give directions.

MP3 08-1

Dialogue 1: On the street

Man	**Excuse me! I'm lost. Could you tell me how to** get to the nearest subway**?**
Woman	Sure. Go straight forward for three **blocks**, then turn right. Walk one more block and the subway will be at the **crossroads. You can't miss it!**
Man	Thank you!
Woman	**You're welcome!**

Dialogue 2: In front of the ticket machine in the subway

Tourist	Oh, excuse me. Could you tell me how to **recharge** my transportation card?
Subway official	Of course. **Place** your card here. Now, **select** the amount of money you want to recharge it for. Okay. Now, **insert** the **bill**. Please wait. Okay, **it's done**. Please take your card. You**'re good to go.**
Tourist	Oh, it was very easy. Thank you very much!
Subway official	You're welcome!

Dialogue 3: In the manager's office

Knock knock!

Manager	Come in! Ah, please **take a seat**. Mr. Kim, I asked you to **drop by** because we haven't received the **urgent** monthly report yet. Could you please send it **ASAP**?
Mr. Kim	Yes, we are very sorry. Please understand. Three employees were off sick for three days, so we've all been **overworked. Would you mind** giving us one extra day**?**
Manager	I understand, but I've got to receive it **by** 6 p.m. tomorrow; **otherwise**, we're all in trouble with the vice chairperson. Give me a call when it's done… and **don't** be late!

Comprehension Check

According to the dialogue, which of the following is correct?

1 Why does the man ask for directions?
   a He's lost his map.   b He's lost his way.   c He's lost his footing.

2 Where does he want to go?
   a the subway closest to his present location
   b the farthest subway   c the subway in this block only

3 What should he do?
   a Firstly, turn right at the next block.   b Firstly, turn right within two blocks.
   c Firstly, turn right after the third block.

4 Where is the subway?
   a across the street   b at the next corner   c at the intersection

5 Where is the tourist?
   a at the turnstile   b at the ticket vending machine
   c at the ticket counter

6 What does the tourist want to do?
   a She wants to refill her transportation card.
   b She wants to buy a one-way ticket.
   c She wants to buy a round-trip ticket.

7 What order of instructions should she follow?
   a place−insert−select   b select−insert−place   c place−select−insert

8 Why did the manager ask Mr. Kim to drop by?
   a The monthly report is postponed.   b The monthly report is well-overdue.
   c The monthly report has been received.

9 What is Mr. Kim's excuse?
   a His workload has been too light.   b His workload has been too tight.
   c His workload has been too trite.

10 When must Mr. Kim send the report?
   a after 6 p.m. tomorrow   b any time before 6 p.m. tomorrow
   c dead on 6 p.m. tomorrow

Useful Expressions

MP3 08-2

Let's learn the meanings and examples of the following expressions.

1	**Excuse me!**	used as a polite way of attracting the attention of a person Ex. Excuse me! Could you tell me the time?
2	**I'm lost.**	I cannot find my way on the street. I don't know the right direction. Ex. "I'm lost, and I can't find my mom," the little girl cried.
3	**Could you tell me how to…?**	an expression used to ask for help Ex. Could you tell me how to use this?
4	**You can't miss it!**	an expression used after giving road directions to say that it is easy to find Ex. Don't worry! It's easy to find! You can't miss it!
5	**You're welcome!**	an expression to say it was a pleasure for you to help Ex. You're welcome. I was happy to help you!
6	**It's done!**	The action is completed. Ex. A: Did you finish the report? B: Yes! It's all done!
7	**be good to go**	be ready or prepared for something Ex. Your paperwork is complete, so you are good to go!
8	**Take a seat!**	a polite way to ask someone to sit down Ex. Good morning, Mr. Fox! Please take a seat.
9	**ASAP**	as soon as possible Ex. Don't worry. I know we don't have much time. I'll contact you ASAP.
10	**Would you mind + verb + -ing?**	used to ask someone politely to do something Ex. Would you mind sending me an update on the meeting you had recently?
11	**be overworked**	have way too much work in contrast to one's signed contract Ex. Many workers complain that they are overworked.
12	**by…**	used to indicate a time by which an action should be finished Ex. Please send the document by Friday midnight. (i.e. the document has a deadline of Friday midnight. It can be sent before, but not after midnight on Friday.)

Grammar

The Imperative Form

A **Usage** The Imperative Form is used to demand or require an action to be performed. It can also be made in a more polite way.

B **Formation** The bare form of the infinitive is used for all subjects.

Infinitive	Imperative	Negative
to come in	Come in!	Don't come in!
to ask	Ask!	Don't ask!
to stop	Stop!	Don't stop!

Note 1 **The above can be made into a more polite or request form:**

Infinitive	Imperative	Negative
to come in	Please come in!	Please don't come in!
to ask	Please ask!	Please don't ask!
to stop	Please stop!	Please don't stop!

Note 2 **If you are included in the advice, request, or order you can say:**

Infinitive	Imperative	Negative
to come in	Let's come go in!*	Let's not come go in!*
to ask	Let's ask!	Let's not ask!
to stop	Let's stop!	Let's not stop!

Note 3 **If you want to ask the question form of the above you can say:**

Infinitive	Imperative	Negative
to come in	Shall we come go in?	Shall we not come go in?*
to ask	Shall we ask?	Shall we not ask?
to stop	Shall we stop?	Shall we not stop?

** **Note** Come changes to Go here because the movement is from where the speaker is to another place.*

Exercise

A   **Fill in the blanks with an appropriate phrase that you learned from the dialogues.**

1   " _____ _____ English only in class," the teacher politely said. (speak)

2   (Knock knock!) "_____ _____ , please!" (come)

3   "Hey! _____ _____ loudly in the library!" the man angrily said to the children. (speak)

4   "Good morning, Ms. Leigh. _____ _____ a seat!" (take)

5   " _____ _____ around the swimming pool. It's slippery." (run)

6   "Damian! _____ _____ loudly on your phone on public transportation," said Damian's dad. (speak)

7   _____ _____ me your address. I need it for the delivery. (give)

8   " _____ up straight. _____ _____ ! It's better for your back," the doctor advised. (sit, slouch)

9   " _____ _____ now! Like that, we can avoid the traffic jam." (go)

10   Be careful _____ to _____ your secret number to others. (show)

B   **Make complete sentences or questions using the prompts.**

1   Excuse me! Could you / the way / the subway station? (tell me)

_____

2   Excuse me! Could you / use / this photocopy machine? (tell me)

_____

3   Could you / the meaning / this sentence? (explain to me)

_____

4   Could you / make / ramen? (show me)

_____

5   Please / the questionnaire / by tomorrow (fill in)

_____

6   Would you mind / earlier / to the office tomorrow morning? (get)

_____

7   Would you mind / the assistant know / the time of your arrival? (let)

_____

8   Could you / how / I / my English? (tell me, improve)

_____

Speaking Activity 1

Work with a partner. One person is A, the other is B. Read the situations then A should ask B for help. B should answer. When you have finished, switch roles.

1. You are in front of your office. A wants to know how to get to the nearest subway station. B gives directions.

   Ex. Go straight for two blocks, then turn left. The subway is there. You can't miss it.

2. A wants to know the way to get to B's office from the entrance.

   Ex. Take the elevator to the 9th floor. Turn right and walk until you get to room 316.

3. A wants to know how to recharge a subway ticket.

   Ex. Insert your card in the little compartment. Select the amount you want then insert the bill and wait. When it's done, take your card.

4. A wants to know the best way to find a new job.

   Ex. There are many job sites. Log onto the site and select the field of work you are qualified for. Check out the list of job descriptions then apply for the ones that suit your qualifications.

5. A wants some tips on how to behave on a date!

   Ex. 1. Be polite.
   2. Be well-groomed.
   3. Listen to your date and show interest.
   4. Be natural. Don't fake to be somebody you are not!

6. A doesn't know how to go to your company cafeteria.

   Ex. Take the elevator to level two basement. The cafeteria is right there.

7. A had a big Christmas company dinner last night and wants to know how to cure a slight hangover.

   Ex. Drink plenty of water. Have a good lunch. Try to go home a little earlier and get a good rest this evening!

8. A is a beginner driver and wants some driving tips.

   Ex. Remember all the rules you learned in driving school. Be always aware of your surroundings. Never use your phone while driving. Respect the road rules.

Speaking Activity 2

Work with a partner and discuss the following questions.

1 Who do you give advice to? Whose advice do you follow most?

_____

_____

2 Describe in detail a time when you were lost, physically or mentally.

_____

_____

3 What is the best piece of advice you have ever received?

_____

_____

 Wrap Up & Guess What?

Remember to use the imperative form when giving advice but also remember to use the polite forms too if appropriate (Go! vs. Please go!)

Tip Your tone of voice is important when we give directions etc. Try not to sound too strict or military in order to avoid offending someone.

Guess what?

What are the three top common places where children get lost?

1 _____

2 _____

3 _____

I'VE BEEN WORKING
IN THIS COMPANY
FOR
TWELVE YEARS.

I've been working in this company for twelve years.

In this unit you will learn how to:
- use the present perfect continuous tense
- use new vocabulary and expressions about daily life

Warm-Up

Pair-work Go into pairs and discuss the following questions.

* Note: Don't worry about your accuracy. Just discuss together!

1

Q **Do you like living in your present city/town? Why? Why not?**

A

Ex. Yes, I do. I like it because it's a very convenient place to live and there are many jobs.

2

Q **How about your present home? Tell me the advantages and disadvantages of it.**

A

Ex. It's easy to get to my office, and there are many good schools for my children. However, it's expensive.

3

Q **When did you come to this company? How satisfied are you with your job? What are the pros and cons?**

A

Ex. I came 5 years ago. I like the location of the company and the fact that I can also work from home. However, I have many deadlines that have to be strictly met.

4

Q **When did you start learning English?**

A

Ex. I started learning English when I was in elementary school.

5

Q **About how long have you been living in this city/town?**

A

Ex. I have been living here for about 12 years.

Vocabulary

A   **Match the word(s) on the left with the definition on the right.**

1 admission	• •	a lately; not long ago
2 elderly	• •	b the act of admitting/accepting
3 my folks	• •	c a term to describe senior citizens of society
4 recently	• •	d working all day (usually, 40 hours or more per week)
5 full-time	• •	e a colloquial term for your parents
6 stable	• •	f the action of finding new people to join an organization
7 graduate from	• •	g not changing, firmly fixed
8 undertaking	• •	h not a stable increase, more and more rapidly
9 recruitment	• •	i complete a course of education
10 exponentially	• •	j a large or difficult task

B   **Fill in the blanks with a word from the box.**

admission	my folks	full-time	stable	graduating from
recruitment	undertaking	recently	elderly	exponentially

1   That school's standard for _____ is high.

2   Special seats on the subway are reserved for _____ passengers.

3   Sometimes _____ _____ and I disagree.

4   They had a hectic schedule _____ preparing for their upcoming marriage.

5   She is currently working as a _____ employee from 8:30 a.m. to 5:30 p.m.

6   The ideal goal is to achieve a _____ economy.

7   After _____ _____ university, it took time to find a stable job.

8   The replacement of the old library was a huge _____.

9   The _____ process to hire new employees will start next month.

10   Social security benefits are growing _____.

Dialogue

The interview at a Korean university for the position of Head of Public Relations' International Admissions.

MP3 **09-1**

Interviewer   Good morning. **Please take a seat.** Let's begin the interview. Could you briefly introduce yourself?

Interviewee   Sure. My name's John William Jones and I'm from the U.S.A. I moved to South Korea about 1 year ago **after marrying** my Korean wife. She wanted to come back to her home country because her parents are very **elderly**. **My folks passed away** when I was young. We have **a newborn baby**, so we have both been very busy taking care of her **recently**. It's been quite hectic. I've been working for some interim agencies since we arrived in Korea, but now I'm looking for a **full-time stable** job.

Interviewer   Your resume says you've been working in public relations. **Could you elaborate on** your work experience so far**?**

Interviewee   Of course. After **graduating from** Berkeley in International Business, I got a job at the university itself in the department of foreign admissions. **I'm fluent in** Chinese and I can also **get by in** Korean, so I have been responsible for all the **undertakings** with the Chinese and South Korean students in their application procedures. I'm still working for them now online, so I've been working with them for two years now. It's just part time, so I've been looking to secure a more reliable full-time position with a Korean university in its **recruitment** of foreign students. So far, I have had a lot of success in my work, and the **admissions'** rate of Asian students at Berkeley has been growing **exponentially** since the end of Covid. I've known a lot of Asian students through my work, and this has been helping me to have better communications with them **from a** cultural **point of view**. Since coming to Korea, I've been trying to improve…

Interviewer   *(The phone rings)* Oh sorry. Just a second please. Somebody has been trying to contact me and it's rather urgent. **Let me** take this call. **Just a minute, please**.

(One minute later)

Sorry about that. So, you were saying that you've been trying to…

Comprehension Check

According to the dialogue, which of the following is correct?

1   What position is John William Jones applying for?
   a   a stable position as University Admissions' officer
   b   sales executive
   c   department head of English language and literature

2   When did he move to Korea?
   a   more than a year ago   b   a year ago   c   a few months ago

3   When did his parents pass away?
   a   when he was a newborn   b   when he was at a young age
   c   when he became an adult

4   What have he and his wife been busy doing recently?
   a   They have been busy taking care of their infant.
   b   They have been busy taking care of their toddler.
   c   They have been busy taking care of their pre-schooler.

5   What has he been doing for a living these days?
   a   living off his savings   b   doing temporary jobs   c   staying at home

6   Where did he graduate from, and what was his major?
   a   He majored in Engineering at Berkeley University.
   b   He majored in International Business at a Korean University.
   c   He majored in International Business at Berkeley University.

7   What are his language skills?
   a   He is tri-lingual.   b   He is mono-lingual.   c   He is bi-lingual.

8   How long has he been working as an interim for Berkeley University?
   a   for two years   b   two years ago   c   in two years

9   What has been happening to the admissions' rate since the end of Covid?
   a   increasing   b   deceasing   c   stabilizing

10   Why does the interviewer have to briefly interrupt the interview?
   a   He should answer an urgent call.
   b   He should make an urgent call.
   c   He should block an urgent call.

Useful Expressions

MP3 09-2

Let's learn the meanings and examples of the following expressions.

1	**Please take a seat.**	a polite imperative asking someone to sit down Ex. You look tired! Please take a seat!
2	**after + verb-ing**	used to show a following sequence Ex. After listening to your advice, I decided to make some changes.
3	**pass away**	a better expression for 'die' when used for other people Ex. Like everyone I will die, but when my beloved grandparents pass away, I will be heartbroken.
4	**a newborn baby**	a baby that is under 28 days old Ex. They took a wonderful photo in the hospital of their newborn baby.
5	**Could you elaborate on...?**	Could you tell me more about...? Ex. Could you elaborate on your opinions about this new project?
6	**be fluent in...**	be able to use something smoothly and without effort (usually a language) Ex. It takes many years of study and practice to be fluent in a foreign language.
7	**get by in...**	be able to survive in a certain situation Ex. I can get by in English in most everyday situations when I travel overseas.
8	**from a ... point of view**	looking at the question in terms of... Ex. From an economic/educational/financial point of view, I think it is good.
9	**Let me + verb**	asking or telling someone that you want/are going to do something Ex. The soup you are making smells delicious. Let me try a bit!
10	**Just a minute, please!**	a polite expression to ask the other person to wait * Note: We don't usually say 'Wait a minute, please!'; we say 'Just a minute, please!' Ex. Just a minute, please! Let me check your boarding pass seat number.

Grammar

The Present Perfect Continuous

A   Usage This tense is used to describe actions that started in the past and continues to the present.

B   Formation

1 Affirmative

Subject	Auxiliary (1&2)	Verb	Object	
I	have(1) been(2)	studying	English	
He/She/(It)	has been	studying	English	
We	have been	studying	English	+ for a long time.*
You	have been	studying	English	
They	have been	studying	English	

> **Note** We need to say the time that this action has been going on. Ex. for ten years, since yesterday, recently etc.

2 Negative

Subject	Auxiliary (1)	Verb	Object	
I	haven't	studied	English	
He/She/(It)	hasn't	studied	English	
We	haven't	studied	English	+ for a long time.
You	haven't	studied	English	
They	haven't	studied	English	

> **Note** We need to use the simple form (haven't p.p.) in the negative. I.E. we usually do not say: I haven't been studying English since yesterday.

3 Interrogative

Auxiliary (1)	Subject	Auxiliary (2)	Verb	Object	
Have	you	been	studying	English	
Has	he/she/(it)	been	studying	English	
Have	you	been	studying	English	+ for a long time?
Have	you	been	studying	English	
Have	you	been	studying	English	

Exercise

A **Choose the appropriate phrase that you learned from the dialogue.**

1 My great grandparents (passed away / passed by) before I was born.

2 After (graduating by / graduating from) university, I tried hard to find a job.

3 My next-door neighbors have a (newly / newborn) baby, and it cries all night long!

4 From a (financial / ecological) point of view, most people are having a hard time due to high prices.

5 (Wait / Just) a minute, please. I've got an urgent call.

6 Could you (elaborate / economize) on your work experience?

7 Come in! Please take a (sit / seat).

8 I'm not fluent in Chinese, but I can get (by / on) in Korean.

9 My sister is working for an (interim / stable) agency right now until she finds a new job.

10 This project was a huge (undertaking / undertaker)!

B **Make a sentence/question with the following prompts using the present perfect continuous.**

1 I / work here / 2020

_____

2 How long / you / live / this city?

_____

3 Have you / learn English / a long time?

_____

4 I / work / this company / since 2003.

_____

5 How long / you / wear / that hairstyle?

_____

Speaking Activity 1

Work with a partner and answer the following questions.

1 **How long have you been learning English?**

Ex. I've been learning English for a long time!

2 **What new activity have you been doing recently?**

Ex. Recently I've been reading a book on self-improvement.

3 **What haven't you done for a long time?**

Ex. I haven't spent time with my alumni friends because we are all busy.

4 **How long have you been living in your present place?**

Ex. I've been living there for 3 years.

5 **What kinds of thing have you been doing lately?**

Ex. I've been working hard recently.

6 **Describe the biggest project you have been working on these days in your company.**

Ex. My team has been working on innovative sales' strategies.

7 **What is your hobby and how long have you been doing that?**

Ex. I started learning calligraphy and I've been going to class every Saturday for one year.

8 **What haven't you eaten for a long time?**

Ex. I haven't eaten dumplings for a while because I've been on a strict diet.

9 **Who haven't you spoken to for a while?**

Ex. I haven't spoken to my neighbors since last year!

10 **How long have you been sitting here?**

Ex. I've been sitting here since the class began!

Speaking Activity 2

Work with a partner.

1   Tell your partner three things that you have been doing recently, and three things that you haven't done recently. Explain why these things make you happy or unhappy. Try to create a conversation!

Ex.
- I haven't been to the gym recently. I have been working on my company projects a lot, so I haven't had time. I really want to start the gym again.

- I have been waking up earlier these days and I've been walking for one hour before work. I feel much healthier!

Three things that you have been doing recently

1 _____

2 _____

3 _____

Three things that you haven't done recently

1 _____

2 _____

3 _____

 ## Wrap Up & Guess What?

Remember to use 'have been -ing' to talk about actions that started in the past and continue to the present. However, in the negative, remember to use the present perfect simple form. Also remember that some verbs cannot be used in the continuous form.

Ex.   I ~~have been knowing~~ you for a long time.   →   I have known you for a long time.
I ~~have been loving~~ you since I first saw you. →   I have loved you since I first saw you.

Tip   Watch the pronunciation! The second auxiliary in the sentence, 'I have been living in this city for a long time.' is reduced to a short vowel sound bin. I've *bin* living here for a long time.

Guess what?

What is the correct pronunciation for these words:

1 been
2 said
3 Yorkshire /
Cambridgeshire /
Oxfordshire /
Lancashire

I THINK I'LL GO
TO AUSTRALIA
NEXT YEAR
FOR A HOLIDAY!

UNIT 10

AUSTRALIA

I think I'll go to Australia next year for a holiday!

In this unit you will learn how to:

- use the future simple tense 'will' and the future with 'be going to'
- speak about plans that are hopes/intentions, and plans that are more fixed
- use new vocabulary and expressions about daily life

Warm-Up

Pair-work Go into pairs and discuss the following questions.

* Note: Don't worry about your accuracy. Just discuss together!

1

Q **Do you think a lot about the future, or do you mainly live in the present?**

A

Ex. We all must think about our future, but I try to appreciate the present as much as possible.

2

Q **What do you worry about most for the future?**

A

Ex. Like many people, I worry about my financial situation since my kids' education costs are high.

3

Q **What is your plan for this evening?**

A

Ex. Since it's Friday, I will go out for dinner with my friends.

4

Q **Do you plan what you are going to do for the next day?**

A

Ex. Yes. I always write a short plan of the things I am going to do or must do for the next day.

5

Q **When you go out with friends, do you plan for the evening, or do you decide on the spot?**

A

Ex. I like to plan to avoid walking around for hours!

Vocabulary

Match the words on the left with the definitions on the right.

1	miss	•	•	a	money given from the government to people without a job
2	unemployment benefits	•	•	b	wish that a person or something were with you now
3	caravan	•	•	c	difficult, demanding
4	gig	•	•	d	a vehicle that is equipped for living in; a trailer
5	highly respected	•	•	e	be strongly admired; have much esteem for
6	challenging	•	•	f	where a person's money comes from
7	source of income	•	•	g	a small, usually temporary job, performed informally or on demand
8	ace	•	•	h	having no job, not employed
9	unemployed	•	•	i	having to work beyond one's capacity or strength
10	overworked	•	•	j	accomplish something with success

B **Fill in the blanks using an expression from the box.**

miss	highly respected	unemployed	unemployment benefits	gig
aced	Overworked	challenging	source of income	caravan

1   He is a _____ _____ professor at the university.

2   He is currently _____.

3   Everyone needs a _____ _____ _____ to survive.

4   He's got a small _____ as a DJ in a nightclub.

5   _____ employees are not productive for the company.

6   The job was well-paid, but it was very _____.

7   Many people use a _____ for their summer vacations.

8   I _____ the test!

9   In times of high unemployment, many job-seekers rely on

_____ _____.

10   When I travel abroad, I often _____ my home country's food.

Dialogue

A hopefully soon-to-be-married couple (Jay and Jane) visit the hopefully soon-to-be-bride's parents' (Mr. & Mrs. Sharp) house for a get-together. The discussion is typically stressful.

MP3 **10-1**

Mr. Sharp	So, Jay, tell us about your job. We know our daughter has a **highly respected** job in a bank. **What about you?** How do you **make a living**?
Jay	Well, Sir, at the moment I'm between jobs, but I'm going to have an interview tomorrow.
Mr. Sharp	Between jobs? You mean you're **unemployed**? You mean you have no **source of income**?
Jay	Well not exactly, Sir. I've been receiving **unemployment benefits**, but these will stop soon if I don't get a job soon. Thanks to Jane's job, we've been able to **make ends meet**. However, if all goes well, I think I'll **ace** the interview.
Mrs. Sharp	What kind of a job is it, Jay? Where will you work?
Jay	Oh, they are going to tell me about the job tomorrow. Everything**'s up in the air** right now, but the job will be in different places, so I won't be home often. In fact, I'll be away most of the time.
Jane	But that's okay Mom because I'm going to be very busy, too.
Mrs. Sharp	Oh, we know you are **overworked** dear, with your **challenging** position in the bank, but you will **miss** each other, won't you?
Mr. Sharp	Yes, and not only that, but where are you going to live?
Jane	Well, if Jay gets this **gig** tomorrow, he will have to be in different places all the time. Therefore, we'll rent a **caravan**, and we will all travel around together!
Mrs. Sharp	All? What do mean by 'all'? Are you going to live with his parents in the caravan?
Jay	Ah no, Mrs. Sharp. **As a matter of fact**, we are going to have a baby!
Jane	Yes, Mom and Dad!!! Guess what? You are going to be grandparents. I am going to be very busy taking care of the baby so I'm going to quit my job!
Mr. & Mrs. Sharp	A baby?! Grandparents?! **What a** wonderful surprise!

Comprehension Check

According to the dialogue, which of the following is correct?

1   Why do you think Mr. & Mrs. Sharp are proud of their daughter?
    a   She has a job in a field that many people admire.
    b   She highly respects many people.
    c   She is disrespectful to her bank.

2   What is Jay's current job situation?
    a   He cannot decide between two companies to work for.
    b   He is hunting for a job.
    c   He works between two companies.

3   What has he been receiving?
    a   company perks   b   welfare benefits   c   sales commission

4   Why have they been able to make ends meet?
    a   thanks to Jane's parents' financial help
    b   thanks to Jane's salary
    c   thanks to his inheritance

5   How does Jay feel about tomorrow's interview?
    a   He is optimistic.   b   He is pessimistic.   c   He is skeptical.

6   Why doesn't he know about the type of job he can get?
    a   Nothing has been decided yet about the type of job.
    b   He hasn't decided yet.
    c   They will tell him about the job sometime after the interview.

7   If Jay gets the job, what will they do?
    a   buy a mobile home   b   buy a trailer   c   rent a caravan

8   What is going to happen almost for sure?
    a   They are going to be residentially challenged.
    b   They are going to give their parents a grandchild.
    c   They are going to live happily ever after.

9   What are Jay and Jane going to do in the near future?
    a   follow his work around   b   stay put   c   keep the status quo

Useful Expressions

Let's learn the meanings and examples of the following expressions.

1	**What about you?**	a phrase used to ask the same question or refer to the same idea as was previously said Ex. I loved that movie! What about you?
2	**make a living**	earn enough money to live on Ex. They work as freelancers, but they make a good living.
3	**make ends meet**	manage to make just enough money to live on Ex. It was hard for them to make ends meet since both were unemployed.
4	**be up in the air**	an idea or a project that is open to change; not fixed Ex. This deal is still up in the air. We hope to sign the contract soon.
5	**as a matter of fact**	actually, to say things clearly Ex. As a matter of fact, there are three clients interested in this project.
6	**What a…!**	an exclamatory sentence used to show surprise or amazement at something* Count Nouns: What a nice pen! What a great company! What an interesting meeting! Non-count Nouns / Plurals: What clean water! What lovely hair! What polite children! * Note: We need the article for singular nouns, but we need to omit the article for plural or non-count nouns.

Grammar 1

The Future Simple (Will)

A Usage The future simple tense is used to express intentions for the future. This intention is slightly dependent on a condition which is expressed in the 'if/when/as soon as' clause that is used in the present simple tense.

Ex. I'll call you this evening (if I have time).

B Formation

1 Affirmative

Subject	Auxiliary	Verb	Object	+	Dependent clause
I	will	speak	English		if I study hard.
He/She/(It)	will	speak	English		if he/she/(it) studies hard.
We	will	speak	English		if we study hard.
You	will	speak	English		if you study hard.
They	will	speak	English		if they study hard.

Note The dependent clause is either said or understood (implied) in all the forms (affirmative, negative, and interrogative).

2 Negative

Subject	Auxiliary	Verb	Object	+	Dependent clause
I	will not (= won't)	speak	English		if I do not (= don't) study hard.
He/She/(It)	will not (= won't)	speak	English		if he/she/(it) does not (= doesn't) study hard.
We	will not (= won't)	speak	English		if we do not (= don't) study hard.
You	will not (= won't)	speak	English		if you do not (= don't) study hard.
They	will not (= won't)	speak	English		if they do not (= don't) study hard.

3 Interrogative

Auxiliary	Subject	Verb	Object	+	Dependent clause
Will	I	speak	English		if I study hard?
Will	he/she/(it)	speak	English		if he/she/(it) studies hard?
Will	we	speak	English		if we study hard?
Will	you	speak	English		if you study hard?
Will	they	speak	English		if they study hard?

Grammar 2

The Future With Be Going to

A **Usage** **The future with be going to is used for future actions that have already been planned, or for predictions that seem very likely to happen based on evidence.**

Ex. I'm going to go to Jeju Island this weekend; I got my ticket this morning.

The plane is going to take off in a few seconds. (i.e. it's already speeding on the runway)

B **Formation**

1 Affirmative

Subject	Auxiliary	going to + Verb	Object
I	am	going to take	a vacation.
He/She/(It)	is	going to take	a vacation.
We	are	going to take	a vacation.
You	are	going to take	a vacation.
They	are	going to take	a vacation.

2 Negative

Subject	Auxiliary	going to + Verb	Object
I	am (= I'm) not	going to take	a vacation.
He/She/(It)	is not (= isn't)	going to take	a vacation.
We	are not (= aren't)	going to take	a vacation.
You	are not (= aren't)	going to take	a vacation.
They	are not (= aren't)	going to take	a vacation.

3 Interrogative

Auxiliary	Subject	going to + Verb	Object
Am	I	going to take	a vacation?
Is	he/she/(it)	going to take	a vacation?
Are	we	going to take	a vacation?
Are	you	going to take	a vacation?
Are	they	going to take	a vacation?

Exercise

A **Fill in the blanks with an appropriate word/phrase that you learned from the dialogue.**

1 I think I _____ this exam. It was exactly the question I wanted.

2 In the economic downturn, it is difficult for many people to _____ _____ _____.

3 While I was traveling outside of Korea, I really _____ kimchi.

4 I live in Seoul. _____ _____ _____?

5 The job is well-paid, but it is very _____.

6 Nothing has been decided yet. It's all _____ _____ _____ _____!

7 While looking for a job, they relied on _____ _____.

8 A: Do you like your job?
   B: _____ _____ _____ _____ _____, I love it!

9 He found a fun _____ working as Santa Claus in a department store.

10 My cousin _____ _____ _____ as a free-lance writer.

B **Make a sentence or question with the following words using either the future simple or be going to.**

1 I / call you tomorrow / have time

_____

2 If / the weather / good / we / picnic

_____

3 As soon as I / receive / your address / I / send / the package

_____

4 It / rain! / Look at the black clouds!

_____

5 Look! / The plane is coming in / It / land / soon

_____

6 If I tell you my secret, you / tell me / yours?

_____

7 We / not / go / India. / All the planes have been canceled.

_____

8 As soon as / receive / your documents / we / write / the contract

_____

Speaking Activity 1

Work with a partner and answer the following questions using the two future tenses you have learned in this unit.

1 Do you have plans for this weekend? What do you think you will do?

> Ex. I have no plans. I think I will stay home all weekend.

2 Where are you going to go this evening?

> Ex. I am going to go back home.

3 What is one sure thing that is going to happen today?

> Ex. The sun is going to set today at 17:54.
> My kids are not going to finish all their homework before 7 p.m.
> They have too much to do.

4 If you have enough time this weekend, what will you do?

> Ex. I'll go to the movies, or I'll go to the sauna and take some rest.

5 Tell me two of your fixed plans.

> Ex. I'm going to go to Japan next month on a business trip.
> My family and I are going to move house next month.

6 Where do you think you will live after you retire?

> Ex. I think I'll live in this same city because all my friends and
> family will continue living here too.

7 Do you think the economy will improve soon? Why/why not?

> Ex. I think and hope it will improve from next year since experts have
> predicted a better job market in the coming years.

8 Tell me something that you are definitely not going to do this evening.

> Ex. I am definitely not going to stay out late partying with friends.
> I am very tired today.

9 If you have children, what do you hope they will do in the future?

> Ex. Firstly, I hope my children will be happy. Secondly, I hope they will
> get a good job that they like, and thirdly, I hope they will become
> wise through good life experiences.

Speaking Activity 2

Work with a partner.

1   Tell your partner how you think your country will change in the future. Think about some of the following:

- Education
- The Environment

- Politics
- People's health

- Food
- Relationships/marriage/the birth rate

_____

_____

_____

_____

_____

 Wrap Up & Guess What?

Remember to use 'will' for future intentions, and 'be going to' for already made plans or actions that are almost inevitable.

Tip Remember that the pronunciation of 'I'm going to' is sometimes pronounced as 'I'm gonna', but this is informal. Know when to use the full pronunciation (going to) and the reduced form (gonna).

Guess what?

What do these English phrases mean? What will they do according to superstition?

1 fingers crossed
2 touch wood

Cultural Tidbits on Dating and Marriage

1   <u>Meeting places</u>. In America and western Europe, people usually meet in bars/pubs, clubs, universities, or dating apps. It is not usual to go to a 'matchmaking' agency to find your future spouse.

2   <u>P.D.A.</u> (public displays of affection) It is frequent to see couples hugging and kissing each other on the street, or on park benches.

3   <u>Age</u>. Although couples are usually around the same age it is also possible for there to be a large age gap between the two, no matter the gender.

4   <u>Co-habitation</u>. Living together before marriage, or living together without marriage is quite common, especially if the couple has no children.

5   <u>Wedding guests</u>. The guests at a wedding are usually family, close friends, and friends. Co-workers, and friends of the parents, or people the bride and groom do not really know are not usually invited.

6   <u>Gifts</u>. Money is not given as a gift. The bride and groom prepare a wedding gift list with a range of items and prices, and it is sent to the guests who choose the gift they want to give. The more expensive items are usually reserved for family or very close friends.

7   <u>Carrying over the threshold</u>. It is usual practice for the man to carry the bride over the threshold of their new home the first time they both enter it.

8   <u>Reasons for marriage</u>. Top on the list for getting married is love (88%), followed by companionship (76%), having children (49%), financial stability (28%), and legal rights and benefits (23%).

– Pew Research Center

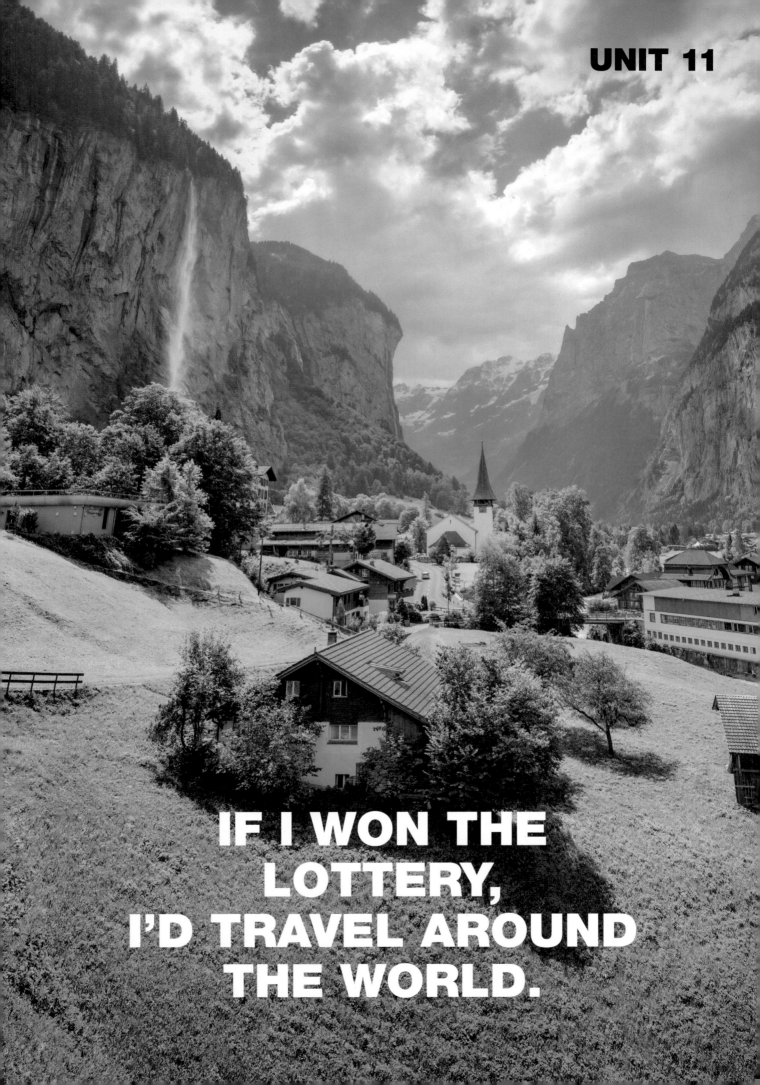

IF I WON THE LOTTERY, I'D TRAVEL AROUND THE WORLD.

If I won the lottery, I'd travel around the world.

In this unit, you will learn how to:

- use the present conditional tense in English
- speak about imaginary situations that could possibly become real
- use new vocabulary and expressions about daily life

Warm-Up

Pair-work Go into pairs and discuss the following questions.

* Note: Don't worry about your accuracy. Just discuss together!

1

Q **When do you mostly daydream?**

A

Ex. I daydream when I'm on public transportation, or when I drive back home after work.

2

Q **What are some of the things that people daydream about?**

A

Ex. I think they daydream about changing jobs, traveling, becoming richer, their children's future etc.

3

Q **What helps us to daydream?**

A

Ex. I think movies, advertisements, music, or maybe a few glasses of wine help us to go into the world of dream!

4

Q **What is your biggest dream when you were a child?**

A

Ex. I dreamed about becoming the President, a singer, an athlete, a designer etc.

5

Q **What is your number one dream right now?**

A

Ex. My number one dream right now is to move to a bigger apartment or...to lose 5 kilos!

Vocabulary

A Match the word on the left with its definition on the right.

1 bump into •	• a	meet someone by chance; drive your car into another vehicle (not usually very serious)
2 the odds •	• b	stop doing something that is difficult or unpleasant
3 quit •	• c	a kiosk on the street that sells newspapers, light refreshments, and chocolate bars
4 dead end •	• d	going nowhere, not leading to anything else
5 consult •	• e	the chances that something will likely happen
6 newsstand •	• f	ask for guidance from a specialist
7 tropical •	• g	selling numbered tickets and giving money prizes to those holders whose tickets are drawn out
8 awesome •	• h	of, typical of, or peculiar to the tropics, very hot and humid climates
9 let go of •	• i	allow someone or something to go free, abandon, stop all contact with someone
10 lottery ticket •	• j	wonderful

B Fill in the blanks with an expression from the box.

lottery ticket	dead-end	let go of	awesome	bump into
The odds	quit	consulted	tropical	newsstand

1 Many people buy a _____ _____ every week.

2 _____ _____ of success for this project are high.

3 He _____ smoking three years ago.

4 This is a _____ road.

5 The company _____ an attorney to deal with the claim.

6 The little boy _____ _____ _____ his mom's hand in the mall.

7 In cool climates, some _____ plants need to be grown in greenhouses.

8 The Moon landing by NASA was _____.

9 I usually buy my morning newspaper at a _____ near my work.

10 It is rare to _____ _____ a friend while traveling abroad.

Dialogue

Two co-workers **bump into** each other in front of a street **newsstand** in the early Monday morning.

MP3 **11-1**

Beth	Oh! Jay! **What a surprise!** What are you doing here? I'm just buying my morning newspaper.
Jay	*(nervously)* Ah Beth! Well…**promise not to tell**, but I'm buying my weekly **lottery ticket**.
Beth	*(laughing)* Oh, you**'ve got nothing to hide**, but do you seriously believe in that?!
Jay	Yeah, I know **the odds** of winning are low, but I just **try my luck** every week! You never know! Someone has to win. That someone could be me. Shall I buy you a ticket? We'll share the millions of dollars if we win.
Beth	If we win! I think you mean we would share the millions of dollars if we won. Do you realize that the chances of winning are as high as **being struck by lightning** which means almost impossible? I would never believe in winning even if you bought me the ticket.
Jay	Well, I offered! If I win, I won't give you any part of the winning money! I'll **keep it** all **to myself**.
Beth	You mean if you won, you would keep it all to yourself!!! Anyway, tell me. What would you do if you won a lot of money?
Jay	Well **for a start**, I'd **quit** my **dead-end** job and I'd open my own online business in management **consulting**. Then I'd leave my ridiculously small and expensive apartment and if I won enough, I'd buy a yacht and travel around the world. Then, I would do my work **from the comfort of my** luxurious yacht. I'd probably work about 1 to 2 hours a day and I'd spend most of the time swimming and drinking champagne.
Beth	Would you **let go of** all your friends?
Jay	Sure, I would. Who would need friends? I would have the **tropical** scenery, the ocean, the birds. That would be enough for me.
Beth	Well, it sounds **awesome**, and **I wish you the best of luck**. I really hope you win. Oh, look at the time. It's almost 9 a.m. Time to get into the office.
Jay	Yep! **Back to the real world!** Bye!
Beth	Dream on, Jay! Bye! *(talking to the newsstand seller)* A lottery ticket, please!

Comprehension Check

According to the dialogue, which of the following is correct?

1   Where do Beth and Jay bump into each other?
    a in front of a shop   b in front of a hotel   c in front of a street stand

2   What is Beth buying? How about Jay?
    a She is buying her morning coffee, and he is buying the weekly lottery ticket.
    b She is buying a newspaper, and he is collecting his lottery ticket win.
    c She is buying a newspaper, and he is betting on a lottery ticket win.

3   How often does Jay buy a lottery ticket?
    a daily   b weekly   c monthly

4   What does Jay know about his chances of winning?
    a The odds are high.
    b The odds are low.
    c The possibility of winning is a tie.

5   Why does he keep on buying the lottery ticket?
    a He trusts in luck.
    b He believes he is unlucky.
    c He doubts his luck.

6   How does Beth feel about the chances of winning the lottery?
    a She is highly skeptical.
    b She is highly optimistic.
    c She is highly confident.

7   What is the first thing Jay would do if he won the lottery?
    a quit his promising career at the company
    b quit his highly lucrative job at the company
    c quit his highly unsatisfactory job at the company

8   How would he spend his days?
    a enjoying nature in a solitary life
    b enjoying a hectic professional life
    c enjoying the city's night scene

Useful Expressions

MP3 **11-2**

Let's learn the meanings and examples of the following expressions.

1	**What a surprise!**	an expression to show an unexpected event
		Ex. I never thought you would remember my birthday! What a surprise!
2	**Promise not to tell!**	an expression to ask someone to keep what you are about to say as a secret
		Ex. Promise not to tell, but I've just got/gotten a pay raise.
3	**have nothing to hide**	an expression to say that a person or company is legal or not doing anything wrong
		Ex. The company had nothing to hide and was willing to show all the necessary documents in court.
4	**try one's luck**	see if one can be lucky
		Ex. I'll try my luck at this difficult job interview tomorrow.
5	**be struck by lightning**	a flash of electrical current from the clouds hitting a person or thing on the ground
		Ex. In the case of a storm, it is not good to stand under a tree for fear of being struck by lightning.
6	**keep something to yourself**	keep something a secret
		Ex. There is a rumor that we will be getting a raise but keep it to yourself since I don't know if it's true or not.
7	**for a start**	to top the list
		Ex. I can no longer live in my present apartment. For a start, the inter-floor noise is unbearable.
8	**from the comfort of one's (own) home**	doing something easily and comfortably from one's own home
		Ex. Many people do online grocery shopping from the comfort of their own home.
9	**I wish you the best of luck.**	tell someone that you want everything to be successful
		Ex. I wish you the best of luck in your new position in the company!
10	**back to the real world**	an expression to say that after dreaming, one must now go back to everyday life
		Ex. That Marvel movie was great, but tomorrow is Monday and so we must go back to the real world!

Grammar

The Present Conditional

A **Usage** This tense (would do) is used to speak about actions or happenings that we can dream about or are hypothetical. It is used with the 'if' clause which is in the past simple tense (did).

Ex. I would buy a house if I had enough money.

B **Formation**

1 Affirmative

Subject	Auxiliary	Verb	Object	
I	would	speak	English	
He/She/(It)	would	speak	English	
We	would	speak	English	+ if I/he/she/(it)/we/you/they studied hard.
You	would	speak	English	
They	would	speak	English	

2 Negative

Subject	Auxiliary	Verb	Object	
I	wouldn't	speak	English	
He/She/It	wouldn't	speak	English	
We	wouldn't	speak	English	+ if I/he/she/we/you/they studied less.
You	wouldn't	speak	English	
They	wouldn't	speak	English	

3 Interrogative

Auxiliary	Subject	Verb	Object	
Would	you	speak	English	
Would	he/she/(it)	speak	English	
Would	we	speak	English	+ if I/he/she/(it)/we/you/they studied hard?
Would	you	speak	English	
Would	they	speak	English	

Exercise

A   **Fill in the blanks with an appropriate phrase that you learned from the dialogue.**

1   My great grandparents buy a _____ _____ every week.

2   I usually buy my newspaper at the _____ on the street.

3   I placed a bet on that horse, even though the _____ of winning were very low.

4   _____ _____ ____ _____, but I'm getting promoted next month!

5   I like to watch movies _____ _____ _____ _____ my own home rather than the movie theatre.

6   A: Why do you like your job?

     B: _____ _____ _____, the work is interesting!

7   Unfortunately, a taxi _____ _____ my car this morning!

8   We can't access the main highway from here because this road is a _____ _____.

9   When did you _____ your former job?

10   I wish you _____ _____ _____ _____ in your new position in this company.

B   **Make a sentence with the following prompts in the present conditional tense.**

1   If you / more money / where / live? (have or earn)

_____

2   Profits / increase / if / they / better factory equipment (have)

_____

3   What / you / do / if / your job? (lose)

_____

4   What / you / do / if / 100 dollars / on the street? (find)

_____

5   Ideally, / what time / wake up / in the morning? (like)

_____

Speaking Activity 1

Work with a partner and answer the following questions.

1 ### Where would you like to live and why?

Ex. I would like to live on Jeju Island because it is my hometown.

2 ### What would you do if you found 100,000 won on the street?

Ex. I would ignore it.

3 ### If you could talk to any famous person (living or dead) who would it be?

Ex. I would talk to Neil Armstrong.

4 ### If you had a much bigger house, what would you use the rooms for?

Ex. I would make a sing-song room, and a movie theatre room.

5 ### If you could choose anywhere, where would you like to be?

Ex. I would like to be in a warm sauna because it is cold today.

6 ### What would be better for you? To live in a hot and humid climate or a cold and damp climate?

Ex. I would prefer to live in a cold and damp climate because I dislike hot and muggy weather.

7 ### If you didn't care about diet and health, what food would you eat this lunchtime?

Ex. I would eat cheese spaghetti with baguette.

8 ### If you gave money to a charity, which one would you give to and why?

Ex. My grandfather died of cancer, so I would give to cancer research.

9 ### If you had a disagreement with your boss, what would you do?

Ex. I would sit down with him/her and try to solve the problem amicably.

10 ### If you were given the chance, would you accept to go to the Moon? Why? Why not?

Ex. Yes. I would love to go to the Moon if I had the chance. I would love to see the image of Earth from the Moon.

Speaking Activity 2

Work with a partner.

1   Tell your partner three things that are your personal dreams right now.

Ex. If I got up earlier, I would go to the gym.
     If my children studied harder, they would get better grades.
     If my company fired me, I would be broke.

1 _____

_____

2 _____

_____

3 _____

_____

☞ Wrap Up & Guess What?

Remember to use 'would do + if + past tense' to speak about ideas that are dreams. There is a possibility that they can happen, but the possibility is very low.

Tip Be careful not to confuse I'd go (= I would go), with I'd gone (= I had gone).

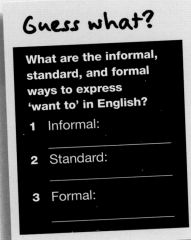

Guess what?

What are the informal, standard, and formal ways to express 'want to' in English?

1 Informal:

_____

2 Standard:

_____

3 Formal:

_____

THE
MEETING
WILL BE
HELD IN THE
CONFERENCE ROOM.

The meeting will be held in the conference room.

In this unit, you will learn how to:

- use the passive voice in English
- sound more professional in your emails and presentations
- use new vocabulary and expressions about daily and professional life

Warm-Up

Pair-work Go into pairs and discuss the following questions.

* Note: Don't worry about your accuracy. Just discuss together!

1

Q **How often do you write emails in English?**

A

Ex. I sometimes have to send English emails to our overseas companies.

2

Q **How often do you give presentations? Do you ever give them in English?**

A

Ex. I often give presentations in Korean except for when I go overseas, and they make me nervous!

3

Q **Do you prefer sending emails/text messages or making voice calls?**

A

Ex. I prefer calling because I can feel the mood of the conversation better.

4

Q **In your opinion, what is the most difficult for you in English?**

A

Ex. My listening skills are not good, especially if the person speaks quickly.

5

Q **How do you feel about movies in which there are a lot of curse words?**

A

Ex. Personally, I think it is not good and I don't want my children to listen to those either.

Vocabulary

A   **Match the word on the left with its definition on the right.**

1   agent •   • a   an identification code
2   C'mon! (= Come on!) •   • b   (informal) used to express dissatisfaction, impatience, or disbelief
3   tracking number •   • c   a person who acts on behalf of another or company
4   inquire •   • d   complain about something in an aggressive way
5   grumble •   • e   a person who handles or deals with a particular object
6   bullet •   • f   formally ask for information from someone
7   last name •   • g   your name derived from your family
8   dispatch •   • h   very fast (when used as an adjective)
9   handler •   • i   send off to a destination
10 customs •   • j   the place at the airport where officials check incoming passengers' luggage

B   **Fill in the blanks with a word from the box.**

| last names | agent | grumbles | bullet | dispatched |
| tracking number | C'mon | handlers | inquire | Customs |

1   The interim company _____ offered her a good position in a top company.

2   _____! You can't be serious!

3   People choose the _____ trains because they are time saving.

4   Good afternoon. I'd like to _____ about the train schedule to Busan.

5   Park, Kim, Lee, Shin, Cho etc. are typical _____ _____ in South Korea.

6   Please have your _____ _____ ready to give to the agent.

7   My grandpa always _____ about the food.

8   An ambulance was _____ immediately.

9   The company is hiring fit and strong workers as factory _____.

10 We went through _____ without any problems since we had nothing to declare.

Dialogue

An online shopper is worried that her package has still not arrived and calls the online company.

MP3 **12-1**

*OSC(= Online Shopping Company), J.G.(= Jenny Grumble), CSR(= Customer Service Representative)

OSC **Please hold the line.** An **agent** will take your call shortly…Please hold the line. An agent will take your call shortly…Please hold the line. An agent will take your call shortly…

J.G. **C'mon!! I don't have all day!** Let's go!

CSR Good morning. This is *Bullet Online Shopping Company*. **How may I help you?**

J.G. Ah, good morning. **I'm calling to inquire** about my 6-foot fake Christmas tree which I ordered 2 months ago. Your company said that it would be delivered between December 1st and the 12th, but it's December 23rd and it still hasn't been delivered. **What on earth**'s happening to my package? Christmas will be over soon so **what's the point of** having a Christmas tree after Christmas**?**

CSR I'm very sorry to hear that, Ma'am. Could you give me your **last name**, and your **tracking number**?

J.G. Yes, it's **Grumble**, Jenny Grumble, and the tracking number is 999 19 911. It looks like a joke but I'm **dead serious**. That's what is written on my receipt.

CSR Thank you. Let me check, please. Ah yes, it was ordered on Halloween, October 31st. According to our records, Ma'am, it was **dispatched** on November 15th, and it is currently **being held up** at **Customs** due to a **handlers**' strike. All package deliveries have been put on hold until a salary increase has been accepted.

J.G. Are you kidding me? My kids will kill me! I told them their Christmas tree will be delivered for sure by Christmas!

CSR Again, I'm very sorry Ma'am but **it's out of our hands** now. How about going to the airport to pick it up yourself?

J.G. You gotta be joking! It's a 30-mile drive to the airport and traffic will be held up due to the holidays! What a nightmare!

CSR **I'm** terribly **sorry for your inconvenience, Ma'am.** Have a Merry Christmas!

Comprehension Check

According to the dialogue, which of the following is correct?

1   What does the online shopping company keep saying?
    a Hold on, please.   b Hold up, please.   c Hold the line, please.

2   What did the customer order?
    a a 6-inch fake Christmas tree
    b a 6-foot artificial Christmas tree
    c a 6-foot real pine Christmas tree

3   When did they say it would be delivered?
    a by December 20th
    b on December 23rd
    c within the first 12 days of December

4   Why is Jenny grumbling?
    a Her Christmas tree is lost in transit.
    b Her Christmas tree is damaged.
    c Her Christmas tree is 11 days late.

5   What does the agent ask for?
    a her first name and identification code
    b her family name and identification code
    c her first name and tracking number

6   When was the Christmas tree ordered?
    a Easter   b Oct 31st   c the eve of Halloween

7   What is happening to the package right now?
    a The package is being held up due to the handlers' sickness.
    b The package is being checked due to the handlers' strike.
    c The package is being delayed because of the handlers' walkout.

8   When will the package be delivered?
    a after the handlers get well again
    b after the handlers get a pay raise
    c after the salary increase has been scrapped

9   What does the agent suggest?
    a going to the airport to pick it up
    b going to the airport to drop it off
    c going to the airport to pick it out

Useful Expressions

MP3 **12-2**

Let's learn the meanings and examples of the following expressions.

1	**Hold the line, please.**	a professional expression used on the phone to ask someone to wait Ex. Hold the line, please. I will check the information.
2	**I don't have all day!**	an informal/impolite expression used to show that you are in a hurry Ex. (In a traffic jam shouting out of the car window) Hey! Move it! I don't have all day!
3	**How may I help you?**	(professional and formal) an expression used by a customer service person to a client asking in what way they can be of help Ex. Good morning, Ma'am. How may I help you?
4	**I'm calling/ writing to...**	used over the phone or in an email to give the reason why you are calling or sending the email Ex. I'm calling to ask about your hotel room prices.
5	**What on earth...**	an expression used to show complete surprise Ex. What on earth did they do to this hotel? It looked much better before the remodelling!
6	**What's the point of...?**	a surprised expression used to ask the reason for something Ex. What's the point of going to the movies when you can download a movie and watch it from the comfort of your own home?
7	**dead serious**	completely serious and not joking at all Ex. The CEO was dead serious when he told us we would all get a bonus at the end of the year because as you see, we have got it!
8	**be held up**	be in a state of not moving forward Ex. Highway traffic was held up due to construction work.
9	**It's out of my/ our hands.**	I/we can no longer do anything about it. The responsibility is on others. Ex. The case will go to the Ministry of Financing. It is now out of our hands.
10	**I am sorry for your inconvenience, Ma'am/Sir.**	a polite expression used in business to show apologies for a client's difficult situation Ex. I'm sorry for your inconvenience, Sir. We hope you will be satisfied with the new contract conditions.

Grammar

The Passive Voice

A Usage **The passive voice is used for three situations:**

1 When we do not know who did the action

2 When the action is more important than who did the action

3 For more formal style. It is often used in business situations for emails or telephone conversations.

B Formation **The object of the situation becomes the subject. The main verb is put into the past participle. We need the verb 'be' which must be put into the required tense.**

Ex. 1 I send an update report to my boss every day. (active voice)
→ An update report is sent to my boss every day.

Ex. 2 We sent the new photocopy machines last week.
→ The new photocopy machines were sent last week.

The Passive Voice in the 6 tenses studied in this Book:

Active Voice	→	Passive Voice
I send an email.		An email is sent.
I am sending an email.		An email is being sent.
I sent an email.		An email was sent.
I will send an email.		An email will be sent.
I am going to send an email.		An email is going to be sent.
I would send an email.		An email would be sent.

Exercise

A By now, you should know all the irregular verbs by heart. To make the passive voice, your ability to know the past participle of the verb will be essential. Fill in the blanks to double check your knowledge.

irregular verbs

infinitive	past simple	past participle	infinitive	past simple	past participle
1 awake			36 keep		
2 be			37 know		
3 become			38 lay		
4 begin			39 leave		
5 bend			40 lend		
6 bid			41 let		
7 blow			42 lie		
8 break			43 lose		
9 bring			44 make		
10 build			45 mean		
11 buy			46 meet		
12 catch			47 pay		
13 choose			48 put		
14 come			49 read		
15 cost			50 ring		
16 cut			51 run		
17 do			52 say		
18 draw			53 see		
19 drive			54 sell		
20 drink			55 send		
21 eat			56 sing		
22 fall			57 sit		
23 feel			58 sleep		
24 fight			59 speak		
25 find			60 spend		
26 fly			61 stand		
27 forget			62 swim		
28 get			63 take		
29 give			64 teach		
30 go			65 tell		
31 grow			66 think		
32 hang			67 throw		
33 have			68 understand		
34 hear			69 wake		
35 hold			70 win		

B **Put the following into the passive voice.**

1 They speak English in this store.

_____

2 Mr. Kim sent the package two days ago.

_____

3 They founded this company in the late 70s.

_____

4 The teacher will give the exams at the end of the semester.

_____

5 They are doing the construction work right now.

_____

6 Somebody has stolen my bicycle.

_____

7 The company would sell more cars if they used more advanced technology.

_____

8 They pay the salaries at the end of the month.

_____

9 The earthquake has damaged many buildings.

_____

10 She will tell you at the end of the meeting.

_____

C **Use the following prompts to make a passive voice sentence or question. Choose the correct answer.**

1 **My house interior / remodel / last year**
   a My house was remodel last year.
   b My house was remodelled last year.

2 **The manual / print / right now**
   a The manual is printed right now.
   b The manual is being printed right now.

3 **A new bridge over the Han River / build / in 2023**
   a A new bridge built over the Han River in 2023.
   b A new bridge was built over the Han River in 2023.

4 **1,500 cars / sell / so far**
   a 1,500 cars is sold so far.   b 1,500 cars have been sold so far.

5 **This movie / make / 2022**
   a This movie was made in 2022.   b This movie was maked in 2022.

6 **The company promotions / announce / in a few minutes**
   a The company promotions are going to be announced in a few minutes.
   b The company promotions will announce in a few minutes.

7 **Subway fares / raise / next month**
   a Subway fares are going be raised next month.
   b Subway fares are going to be raised next month.

8 **When / you / think / we / give / a raise?**
   a When do you think we will be given a raise?
   b When do you think we will be give a raise?

9 **How many of our products / manufacture / last year?**
   a How many of our products is manufactured last year?
   b How many of our products were manufactured last year?

10 **The new office furniture / send / last Monday**
   a The new office furniture were sent last Monday.
   b The new office furniture was sent last Monday.

Speaking Activity 1

Respond to the following questions using the passive voice.

1   If there were a strong typhoon, what kind of damage would be done in your city/town. (Imagine 3 things) (buildings, cars, streets, trees etc.)

1 _____

2 _____

3 _____

2   What are some of the things that have happened because of Covid 19? (Give 3)

1 _____

2 _____

3 _____

3   What changes have been made to your hometown since you were a child? (Give at least 3)

1 _____

2 _____

3 _____

4   In the future, what advances will be made in Korea? (Try to think of 3)

1 _____

2 _____

3 _____

5   What is being done around you now? What was done yesterday in your office? What will be done or is going to be done tomorrow?

1 _____

2 _____

3 _____

Speaking Activity 2

Work with a partner.

1   Tell your partner about some things that have been done in your office since you arrived, and some things that have not been done.

_____

_____

2   Tell your partner about what you hope will be done tomorrow in your company's work.

_____

_____

3   Finally, tell your partner about what you hope will be done in your apartment/area where you live.

_____

_____

 Wrap Up & Guess What?

Remember to use the passive voice in emails, presentations, and exchanges with clients to sound more professional.

Tip   Remember that English also has different styles;
         it is not only informal style that we often hear in movies.

Guess what?

1   What is the British equivalent of the American 'Ma'am'?

2   What kind of a handshake should we give?

3   What salutations can we use to end an email? Give three.

ANSWER
KEY

UNIT 01

Vocabulary

A

1 b   2 d   3 c   4 a   5 e
6 h   7 f   8 i   9 j   10 g

B

1 lines   2 interim agency
3 variety   4 hectic
5 quiet   6 quite
7 suburbs   8 local
9 female friends   10 single life

Comprehension Check

1 a   2 b   3 c   4 c   5 c
6 b   7 a   8 c   9 c

Exercise

A

1 lives   2 work   3 listen
4 get up   5 goes   6 do / have
7 lives   8 does / go   9 wakes
10 rotates   11 do / go   12 do / work out
13 rises   14 starts   15 does / get to

B

1 I never wake up before 6 a.m.
2 The newspaper always arrives before I get up.
3 Does your family ever go to a sauna?
4 How often do you meet your best friends?
5 What time does your office usually open its doors?

Guess What?

1 phones   2 keys   3 wallets

UNIT 02

A

1 d	2 e	3 a	4 c	5 f
6 b	7 g	8 j	9 h	10 i

B

1 letdown	2 slight
3 mood	4 are honored
5 fiancé	6 get promoted
7 big time	8 draft beer
9 be out of town	10 apologize

Comprehension Check

1 c	2 a	3 a	4 c	5 a
6 c	7 c	8 c	9 c	10 a

Exercise

A

1 is eating	2 are going	3 is raining
4 are / doing	5 am coming	6 Is / watching
7 is having / is going	8 attending	9 am getting
10 is / leaving	11 is happening	12 leaving
13 are / drinking	14 is / working	15 snowing

B

1 My friend is visiting Paris tomorrow.
2 The president is making/giving a speech right now.
3 Some co-workers are getting a promotion next month.
4 I am coming down with the flu.
5 Is it raining now?

Guess What?

1 thumb, pointing finger or index finger, middle finger, ring finger, little finger or pinkie
2 ring finger

UNIT 03

Vocabulary

A

1 c   **2** b   **3** d   **4** a

5 f   **6** g   **7** h   **8** e

B

1 Fancy   **2** Raw fish

3 Ugh   **4** yucky

5 cousins   **6** antibiotics

7 non-identical twins   **8** loads of

Comprehension Check

1 c   **2** b   **3** a   **4** b   **5** c

6 a   **7** c   **8** a   **9** b   **10** a

Exercise

A

1 ordered / was moving   **2** caught   **3** Did / submit

4 sprained / was playing   **5** had   **6** did / have

7 was watching   **8** were / doing   **9** was flying / occurred

10 was talking / called

B

1 I broke my ankle while I was playing football.

2 Two years ago, my friend got married.

3 I was riding the subway when a fire broke out.

4 What were you doing [what did you do] when it started to rain?

5 My cousin was not paying attention when the accident happened.

6 The day before yesterday, the students took the exam.

7 Did you arrive at the airport on time?

8 When did you last go to a fancy restaurant?

Guess What?

1 You might hear people say, 'Did you went?' instead of the correct, 'Did you go?'

2 Be careful with the verbs to lie and to lay, too.
(Your teacher will explain the difference.)

UNIT 04

Vocabulary

A

1 c	**2** a	**3** e	**4** b
5 g	**6** d	**7** h	**8** f

B

1 populated   **2** the Eiffel Tower

3 whereas   **4** asylum

5 a close game   **6** solar system

7 dwarf   **8** Oops

Comprehension Check

1 b	**2** b	**3** c	**4** a	**5** b
6 a	**7** c	**8** b	**9** a	

Exercise

A

1 milder   **2** better   **3** more comfortable

4 hardest   **5** fewer   **6** the least

7 easier   **8** farther   **9** earlier

10 better   **11** the best   **12** steepest

13 ugliest   **14** easiest   **15** more exciting

B

1 My life is easier than before.

2 I bought the best book I could find.

3 I hope to make the most profitable decision to maximize our company's growth.

4 It was the worst policy the government has ever made.

5 I ate more than everybody else.

Guess What?

You may hear some people say more bigger, more cheaper, more easier etc. which is incorrect. However, you can say much bigger, much cheaper, much easier etc. which IS correct.

UNIT 05

Vocabulary

A

1 c	2 b	3 d	4 a	5 f
6 e	7 h	8 g	9 j	10 i

B

1 Actually
2 starter
3 Vinaigrette dressing
4 main courses
5 soup of the day
6 Abalone
7 risotto
8 corkage fee
9 dessert
10 bill

Comprehension Check

1 c	2 a	3 a	4 c	5 c
6 c	7 a	8 b	9 c	10 a

Exercise

A

1 am
2 are supposed
3 miss
4 off chance
5 last-minute
6 go light
7 corkage fee
8 have / bill
9 went Dutch
10 starter / main dish / dessert

B

1 I'd like to order the chicken salad.
2 I'd like the curry, but could you go light on the spices?
3 We've brought our own wine. What is the corkage fee?
4 How would you like your steak? Rare, medium, or well-done?
5 Could we have the bill, please? We are ready to leave.

Guess What?

1 grilled pork belly
2 marinated beef
3 black noodles

Others: rice with vegetables (bibimbap)
steamed rice cakes in sweet and spicy sauce (tteokbokki)

UNIT 06

Vocabulary

A

1 b   2 c   3 a   4 f   5 d

6 e   7 j   8 g   9 e   10 h

B

1 abide by   2 lunatic

3 conservative   4 retired

5 pensioners   6 moron

7 beloved   8 excessive

9 the trimmings   10 bucket list

Comprehension Check

1 c   2 a   3 b   4 c   5 a

6 c   7 b   8 c   9 b   10 c

Exercise

A

infinitive	past simple	past participle	infinitive	past simple	past participle
1 be	was / were	been	36 keep	kept	kept
2 become	became	become	37 know	knew	known
3 begin	began	begun	38 learn	learned	learned
4 break	broke	broken	39 leave	left	left
5 bring	brought	brought	40 lend	lent	lent
6 build	built	built	41 let	let	let
7 burn	burned	burned	42 lose	lost	lost
8 buy	bought	bought	43 make	made	made
9 catch	caught	caught	44 meet	met	met
10 choose	chose	chosen	45 pay	paid	paid
11 come	came	come	46 put	put	put
12 cost	cost	cost	47 read	read	read
13 cut	cut	cut	48 ride	rode	ridden
14 do	did	done	49 run	ran	run
15 draw	drew	drawn	50 say	said	said
16 dream	dreamed	dreamed	51 see	saw	seen
17 drink	drank	drunk	52 sell	sold	sold
18 drive	drove	driven	53 send	sent	sent
19 eat	ate	eaten	54 shut	shut	shut
20 fall	fell	fallen	55 sing	sang	sung

21 feed	fed	fed	56 sit	sat	sat
22 feel	felt	felt	57 sleep	slept	slept
23 find	found	found	58 speak	spoke	spoken
24 fly	flew	flown	59 spend	spent	spent
25 forget	forgot	forgotten	60 swim	swam	swum
26 freeze	froze	frozen	61 swing	swung	swung
27 get	got	got	62 take	took	taken
28 give	gave	given	63 teach	taught	taught
29 go	went	gone	64 tell	told	told
30 grow	grew	grown	65 think	thought	thought
31 have	had	had	66 throw	threw	thrown
32 hear	heard	heard	67 wake	woke	woken
33 hit	hit	hit	68 wear	wore	wore
34 hold	held	held	69 win	won	won
35 hurt	hurt	hurt	70 write	wrote	written

B

1 I have already seen the movie.

2 My friend has just gone to the USA.

3 I haven't had lunch yet.

4 Have you ever been to a French restaurant?

5 My parents have never given a presentation.

6 How many times have you visited a sauna in your life so far?

7 Most people have never forgotten their first love.

8 How long have you lived in this country?

9 What have you already eaten today?

10 What have you never done in your life so far?

Guess What?

1 tap   2 truck   3 lift

UNIT 07

Vocabulary

A

1 d	2 c	3 b	4 a	5 g
6 i	7 h	8 j	9 f	10 e

B

1 hectic	2 upturn
3 revenue	4 downturn
5 hardship	6 C'mon
7 executive	8 tighten the belt
9 stress out	10 higher-up

Comprehension Check

1 b	2 b	3 b	4 c	5 a	6 c	7 a

Exercise

A

1 asking	2 getting up	3 ask
4 walking	5 ask	6 take
7 meet	8 call	9 booking
10 stay	11 taking	12 attend
13 sending	14 study	15 do

B

Answers will vary.

Guess What?

MOMS	**GRADUATES**	**DADS**
1 children's education	1 future job	1 job stability
2 family's health	2 marriage	2 money
3 family's financial situation	3 money	3 parents' health

UNIT 08

Vocabulary

A

1 e	2 a	3 d	4 b	5 g
6 c	7 h	8 f	9 j	10 i

B

1 blocks
2 crossroads
3 recharge
4 placed
5 selected
6 insert
7 bill
8 dropped by
9 otherwise
10 urgent

Comprehension Check

1 b	2 a	3 c	4 c	5 b
6 a	7 c	8 b	9 b	10 b

Exercise

A

1 Please speak
2 Come in
3 Don't speak
4 Please take
5 Don't run
6 Don't speak
7 Please give
8 Sit / Don't slouch
9 Let's go
10 not / show

B

1 Excuse me! Could you tell me the way to the subway station?
2 Excuse me! Could you tell me how to use this photocopy machine?
3 Could you explain to me the meaning of this sentence?
4 Could you show me how to make ramen?
5 Please fill in the questionnaire by tomorrow.
6 Would you mind getting earlier to the office tomorrow morning?
7 Would you mind letting the assistant know the time of your arrival?
8 Could you tell me how I can improve my English?

Guess What?

1 theme parks
2 malls
3 parades or outdoor events

UNIT 09

Vocabulary

A

1 b   2 c   3 e   4 a   5 d

6 g   7 i   8 j   9 f   10 h

B

1 admission   2 elderly

3 my folks   4 recently

5 full-time   6 stable

7 graduating from   8 undertaking

9 recruitment   10 exponentially

Comprehension Check

1 a   2 b   3 b   4 a   5 b

6 c   7 c   8 a   9 a   10 a

Exercise

A

1 passed away   2 graduating from   3 newborn

4 financial   5 Just   6 elaborate

7 seat   8 by   9 interim

10 undertaking

B

1 I have been working here since 2020.

2 How long have you been living in this city?

3 Have you been learning English for a long time?

4 I have been working for this company since 2003

5 How long have you been wearing that hairstyle?

Guess What?

1 bin (shortened form)   2 sed (shortened form)

3 shuh (shortened form)

UNIT 10

Vocabulary

A

1 b   2 a   3 d   4 g   5 e
6 c   7 f   8 j   9 h   10 i

B

1 highly respected   2 unemployed
3 source of income   4 gig
5 Overworked   6 challenging
7 caravan   8 aced
9 unemployment benefits   10 miss

Comprehension Check

1 a   2 b   3 b   4 b   5 a
6 a   7 c   8 b   9 a

Exercise

A

1 aced   2 make ends meet   3 missed
4 What/How about you   5 challenging   6 up in the air
7 unemployment benefits   8 As a matter of fact 9 gig
10 makes a living

B

1 I'll call you tomorrow if I have time.
2 If the weather is good, we'll go on a picnic.
3 As soon as I receive your address, I will send the package.
4 It is going to rain! Look at the black clouds!
5 Look! The plane is coming in. It is going to land soon.
6 If I tell you my secret, will you tell me yours?
7 We are not going to India. All the planes have been canceled.
8 As soon as we receive your documents, we will write the contract.

Guess What?

1 Instead of saying, 'Good luck', we say 'Fingers crossed' with the gesture. This is thought to avoid bad luck and bring good luck.
2 'Touch wood'. This is said after a positive statement to hope the positivity will continue.

UNIT 11

Vocabulary

A

1 a   2 e   3 b   4 d   5 f
6 c   7 h   8 j   9 i   10 g

B

1 lottery ticket   2 The odds
3 quit   4 dead-end
5 consulted   6 let go of
7 tropical   8 awesome
9 newsstand   10 bump into

Comprehension Check

1 c   2 c   3 b   4 b   5 a
6 a   7 c   8 a

Exercise

A

1 lottery ticket   2 newsstand
3 odds   4 Promise not to tell
5 from the comfort of   6 For a start
7 bumped into   8 dead end
9 quit   10 the best of luck

B

1 If you had/earned more money, where would you live?
2 Profits would increase if they had better factory equipment.
3 What would you do if you lost your job?
4 What would you do if you found 100 dollars on the street?
5 Ideally, what time would you like to wake up in the morning?

Guess What?

1 Informal: wanna
2 Standard: want to
3 Formal: would like to

UNIT 12

Vocabulary

A

1 c   2 b   3 a   4 f   5 d

6 h   7 g   8 i   9 e   10 j

B

1 agent   2 C'mon

3 bullet   4 inquire

5 last names   6 tracking number

7 grumbles   8 dispatched

9 handlers   10 Customs

Comprehension Check

1 c   2 b   3 c   4 c   5 b

6 b   7 c   8 b   9 a

Exercise

A

infinitive	past simple	past participle	infinitive	past simple	past participle
1 awake	awoke	awoken	36 keep	kept	kept
2 be	was, were	been	37 know	knew	known
3 become	became	become	38 lay	laid	laid
4 begin	began	begun	39 leave	left	left
5 bend	bent	bent	40 lend	lent	lent
6 bid	bid	bid	41 let	let	let
7 blow	blew	blown	42 lie	lay / lied	lain / lied
8 break	broke	broken	43 lose	lost	lost
9 bring	brought	brought	44 make	made	made
10 build	built	built	45 mean	meant	meant
11 buy	bought	bought	46 meet	met	met
12 catch	caught	caught	47 pay	paid	paid
13 choose	chose	chosen	48 put	put	put
14 come	came	come	49 read	read	read
15 cost	cost	cost	50 ring	rang	rung
16 cut	cut	cut	51 run	ran	run
17 do	did	done	52 say	said	said
18 draw	drew	drawn	53 see	saw	seen
19 drive	drove	driven	54 sell	sold	sold
20 drink	drank	drunk	55 send	sent	sent

21 eat	ate	eaten	56 sing	sang	sung
22 fall	fell	fallen	57 sit	sat	sat
23 feel	felt	felt	58 sleep	slept	slept
24 fight	fought	fought	59 speak	spoke	spoken
25 find	found	found	60 spend	spent	spent
26 fly	flew	flown	61 stand	stood	stood
27 forget	forgot	forgotten	62 swim	swam	swum
28 get	got	got (gotten)	63 take	took	taken
29 give	gave	given	64 teach	taught	taught
30 go	went	gone	65 tell	told	told
31 grow	grew	grown	66 think	thought	thought
32 hang	hung	hung	67 throw	threw	thrown
33 have	had	had	68 understand	understood	understood
34 hear	heard	heard	69 wake	woke	woken
35 hold	held	held	70 win	won	won

B

1 English is spoken in this store.

2 The package was sent two days ago.

3 This company was founded in the late 70s.

4 The exams will be given at the end of the semester.

5 The construction work is being done right now.

6 My bicycle has been stolen.

7 More cars would be sold if more advanced technology were used.

8 The salaries are paid at the end of the month.

9 Many buildings have been damaged by the earthquake.

10 You will be told at the end of the meeting.

C

1 b   2 b   3 b   4 b   5 a

6 a   7 b   8 a   9 b   10 b

Guess What?

1 Madam

2 A full firm hand with 2 to 3 shakes

3 1) Sincerely   2) Cordially   3) Best wishes / Warm wishes